D0731457

eating light eating right

eating light eating right

simple recipes for a healthy life

Shauna Ratner, RDN and Frances Johnson, RDN

whitecap

Copyright © 2001 by Providence Health Care
Whitecap Books

Second printing 2002

All rights reserved. No part of this publication may be reproduced, stored
in a retrieval system, or transmitted in any form or by any means, electronic,
mechanical, photocopying, recording or otherwise, without prior written
permission of the publisher.

The information in this book is true and complete to the best of our knowledge.
All recommendations are made without guarantee on the part of the authors or
Whitecap Books Ltd. The authors and publisher disclaim any liability in connection
with the use of this information. For additional information, please contact
Whitecap Books Ltd., 351 Lynn Avenue, North Vancouver, BC V7J 2C4.

Edited by Elaine Jones
Proofread by Elizabeth McLean
Cover design by Roberta Batchelor
Cover photograph by Hot Digital Dog Studios
Cover food styling by J.M. Strongman
Interior design and illustrations by Warren Clark

Printed and bound in Canada

National Library of Canada Cataloguing in Publication Data
Ratner, Shauna, 1963–
    Eating Light, Eating Right

    Includes index.
    ISBN 1-55285-277-6

    1. Low-fat diet—Recipes. I. Johnson, Frances, 1953– II. Title.
RM237.7.R37 2001   641.5'638   C2001-910987-3

The publisher acknowledges the support of the Canada Council for the Arts and the
Cultural Services Branch of the Government of British Columbia for our publishing
program. We acknowledge the financial support of the Government of Canada
through the Book Publishing Industry Development Program for our publishing
activities.

contents

acknowledgements

This cookbook has been in the works for a long time and could not have been completed without the help and support of so many people. Foremost, we must acknowledge all those who made this book a reality by sharing their favourite recipes and interesting ideas with us. Their contribution provides the major framework for this book and we would like to thank them for all their support.

We must also recognize the support of St. Paul's Hospital and especially the staff in the Healthy Heart Program who have always promoted our efforts and inspired us to provide sound nutrition education. We would also like to thank Jill Lambert for her vision and encouragement in pursuing this project. Lastly, we could never have completed this cookbook without the patience and support of our families. Michael, Mark, Terumi, Mika, Andrew and Simone—thank you!

preface

Dear Reader,

In the early 1990s, a group of people who started the "old Shaughnessy" (now St. Paul's Hospital) lipid clinic—a place with advice for individuals with high blood cholesterol or other risk factors for heart disease— decided that we could produce our own healthy recipes. Then, week after week we tasted our own and our patients' dishes, selected the favourites and by the mid-1990s our excellent dietitians, Frances Johnson and Shauna Ratner, published this selection under the title *Eating Light and Loving It!*

Initially we thought that the book would be of interest to our patients, their families and friends. However, to our delight it has become a national bestseller with over 15,000 copies sold in two editions.

A healthy diet, along with exercise and smoking cessation are major factors in determining our well-being. Current debate between proponents of high-protein/fat and lower-fat diets is of interest, but until we have conclusive, evidence-based data regarding the former, we should stay with a reasonable lower-fat diet. This book brings you a new selection of easy to prepare, delicious dishes that will truly be your heart's delight!

Bon appetit,

Jiri Frohlich MD, FRCPC

introduction

Here it is, five years since our first cookbook was published. No sooner was that cookbook off the press than clients were asking about the next book—we were overwhelmed! Since that time there have been many new ideas in the management of heart disease, but diet remains the cornerstone of healthy living. Yet despite how much we know about nutrition, it is still sometimes difficult to put that knowledge into action. Thus, our next project began.

The message we got from everyone was quick, healthy and tasty. Everyone is busy juggling work, family and other commitments with precious little time left to think, "Now, what should I cook?" let alone, "What should I cook that's healthy for me?" This collection of recipes was created to help our readers meet their need for healthy, interesting meals that don't take a lot of fussing or too much time to prepare.

We asked participants of the Healthy Heart Program, as well as friends and relatives, to help us out with their favourite recipes. All kinds of interesting recipes were submitted that seemed to fit our needs. So we rolled up our sleeves and started cooking—in between our busy family lives and professional commitments. It has been a wonderful gourmet experience, not only for us, but also for our families and friends. Some meals became a wild and interesting combination of foods that opened our eyes to new ideas and flavours. Others were simply tasty, healthy versions of traditional comfort foods. We have picked our favourites for you, including some from our own recipe files, and we hope you enjoy them as much as we do. We have tried to provide something for every cook—basic recipes for the inexperienced cook as well as innovative recipes and ideas for the seasoned chef.

We hope this cookbook will help you make healthy eating an everyday part of your life. Eat well and enjoy!

Frances Johnson, RDN
Shauna Ratner, RDN

nutrition notes for getting started ...

We are what we eat!

Despite the enormous advances in medicine, it has become ever more apparent that what we eat has a huge impact on determining "what we are."

Without food, we cannot survive. It is the energy and nutrients in food that provide the fuel and catalysts that enable every cell in our bodies to function properly. Furthermore, exactly what those nutrients are can affect how well those cells function. Eating well is really a juggling act that requires some thought and planning to make sure that we are getting all the nutrients we need.

Some background about the heart-healthy diet

Although the impact of diet on heart disease is well recognized, it is not clear exactly what diet is best. The most widely accepted diet has been one that emphasizes cutting down on fat, especially saturated fat, to reduce cholesterol levels in the blood.

Another approach that has been effective is the Mediterranean type of diet. It places less emphasis on reducing the amount of fat in the diet, but encourages making food choices low in saturated fat and rich in alpha-linolenic acid, antioxidants and other phytochemicals.

Other studies have shown that including certain foods along with a healthy diet might be helpful. For example, eating fish twice per week, or including more fruit, vegetables, grains and some nuts, in addition to a low-fat diet, has shown better outcomes in some studies.

So, which diet should we follow? There is likely no one diet that is best for everyone. We are all individuals and our needs vary, depending on such things as our genetic makeup, the foods we enjoy and the kind of lives we lead. Having stated that, though, the best diet, for now, is probably one that includes meals and snacks that incorporate key principles from ALL of these diets.

Balancing the facts

Even though there are different views regarding exactly what the most heart-healthy diet should be, most researchers agree on the following principles.

- Eat less fat, especially saturated fat.
- Increase fibre, especially soluble fibre.
- Eat foods high in phytochemicals.
- Eat a wide variety of foods to ensure adequate vitamins and minerals.
- Go easy on sugar, salt and alcohol.

The following guidelines can give you an idea of how you might try to achieve those principles.

Guidelines for healthy eating

Choose to eat...	*But be careful to...*
Lean meat, poultry or fish up to 6 ounces (180 grams) per day • eat fish 2–3 times per week • replace meat, poultry or fish with a vegetarian entrée, such as legumes or tofu, at least once per week • eat egg whites as you like	• cut off all fat and remove poultry skin • limit high-fat processed meats, such as salami and sausages • avoid organ meats • limit egg yolks to a maximum of 1–3 per week
Skim milk dairy products • use 1% m.f. or skim milk, yogurt and cottage cheese • eat low-fat cheese that is 15% m.f. or less	• limit cream, sour cream, whipping cream and regular cheese
Whole-grain breads, cereals, grains and pasta • eat enough each day to suit your energy needs	• watch the spread on the bread and the sauces on the pasta
Fresh fruits and vegetables • eat plenty each day, choosing a wide variety	• watch the sauces or cooking fats • drink less juice and eat fruit instead

Choose to eat...	But be careful to...
Vegetable oils, soft margarine, peanut butter and salad dressings in small amounts	
• use light salad dressings and light mayonnaise whenever possible	• use oils, margarine and other high-fat spreads sparingly. Remember—"If you don't need it, don't use it."
• choose low-fat condiments, such as mustard, relish, ketchup and salsa	• avoid high-fat creamy sauces
• use tomato-based sauces	• eat nuts and seeds only when you know you can stop after having just a few
Low-fat desserts in moderation, such as angel-food cake, low-fat frozen yogurt, low-fat cookies	
• make homemade loaves and muffins using no more than $1/4$ cup (50 mL) oil or margarine per loaf or dozen muffins	• limit high-fat baked goods, ice cream and chocolates
• remember that the best choice for dessert is fruit	• keep in mind that half of a portion is also half the fat
Low-fat snacks such as pretzels, plain popcorn, baked chips, cereals and fresh fruit	• limit potato chips, corn chips, nuts and other high-fat snack foods
	• remember that too many low-fat snack foods can add up to too many calories!

Basic fat facts

Fat is in most foods, including plant and animal products, and is an important part of our diet. It acts as a carrier for the fat-soluble vitamins A, D, E and K, and can be a major source of energy. It also provides essential fatty acids that are necessary for good health. However, eating too much fat has been linked to health problems, such as heart disease, cancer and obesity.

Sorting out the facts about fat can be confusing because not all fats are the same. A simple way to look at fats, though, is thinking of fats as "good" and "not so good" for controlling heart disease, keeping in mind that we still need fat in general as part of a healthy diet. Dietary fats are made up of a mixture of saturated, monounsaturated and poly-unsaturated fatty acids. Use this guide to help you sort out the fat facts.

Saturated fats are "not so good" and raise blood cholesterol. They are found in largest amounts in meat and dairy products, such as butter, regular cheese and whole milk. Saturated fat is also found in vegetable products, such as coconut and palm oils. *Choose foods low in saturated fats.*

Monounsaturated and polyunsaturated fats are "good" fats and lower cholesterol levels when substituted for saturated fats. Monounsaturated fats are especially high in such oils as olive, canola and peanut oils. Polyunsaturated fats are found mainly in plant products, such as safflower, sunflower, corn and soybean oils. *Choose these unsaturated fats, but be careful not to have too much.*

Omega 3 fatty acids are "good" fats found in fish and some vegetable oils, such as canola and flax. Studies have shown that these fats may help to reduce your risk for heart disease. *Include fish regularly in your diet and choose canola oil in small amounts for cooking.*

Trans fatty acids are "not so good" fats formed by a process called **hydrogenation** when liquid oils are converted to solid fats. These trans fatty acids behave like saturated fats and can increase blood cholesterol. Foods such as vegetable shortening and hard margarine are high in trans fatty acids. *Choose soft non-hydrogenated margarine and liquid vegetable oils in small amounts instead of these hardened fats.*

Cholesterol is not a fat, but a fat-like substance found in foods of animal origin, mainly meat, poultry, fish and dairy products. It is especially high in foods such as egg yolks and organ meats. It is not found in any food that comes from plants. Remember, though, that "cholesterol free" does not mean "fat free." *Enjoy up to 3 egg yolks per week and organ meats just once in a while.*

Balancing your fat budget

Of the food you eat, the total amount of fat eaten should average out to no more than 30% of your overall calorie intake. That means if you were to eat 2000 calories per day, you should eat less than 66 grams of fat each day. Most adults should eat no more than 40 to 80 grams of fat per day, depending on how many calories are usually eaten. The following chart will give you an idea of what your "fat budget" might be.

Calories eaten per day	Daily fat budget
1200 calories	40 grams
1500 calories	50 grams
1800 calories	60 grams
2100 calories	70 grams
2400 calories	80 grams

Going beyond fats

Controlling only how much fat we eat is not enough to ensure a nutritious diet for preventing or controlling heart disease. Research shows that there are a variety of nutrients and phytochemicals that are especially involved in reducing our risk for heart disease. The following are just some of those important components found in food.

Phytochemicals – natural chemicals found in all plants that may fight disease and promote health. These include phytosterols and various antioxidants.

Phytosterols – plant sterols found in plants that can help reduce cholesterol levels in the blood. They are high, especially in corn, soy and other legumes.

Antioxidants – protective substances found in foods that help to protect our bodies from cell damage. Familiar types include vitamins such as beta-carotene, vitamin C and E, and minerals such as selenium. Other antioxidants, such as lycopenes, provide the red colour in tomatoes, while flavonoids are abundant in soy, lentils and other legumes.

Folic acid – a B vitamin that helps to lower homocysteine levels in the blood. High levels of homocysteine may contribute to hardening of the arteries. Beans, asparagus, lentils, spinach, beets, corn and Brussels sprouts are especially high in folic acid.

Fibre – all fibre, or roughage, is important for maintaining regular bowel habits and overall general health. Whole-grain products, fresh fruits and vegetables are high in insoluble fibre. Soluble fibre may play a significant role, especially in heart health, and is abundant in oats, beans and apples.

Remember that simply taking supplements of these food components is not the best answer for maintaining health. Food is a combination of so many minute, yet powerful nutrients, and eating foods that house these important nutrients is absolutely vital for staying healthy.

Eating a well-balanced diet with food choices from all groups in Canada's Food Guide is our best chance for getting all the nutrients our bodies need.

CANADA'S
Food Guide
TO HEALTHY EATING

Enjoy a variety
of foods from each
group every day.

Choose lower-
fat foods
more often.

Grain Products	Vegetables & Fruit	Milk Products	Meat & Alternatives
Choose whole grain and enriched products more often.	Choose dark green and orange vegetables and orange fruit more often.	Choose lower-fat milk products more often.	Choose leaner meats, poultry and fish, as well as dried peas, beans and lentils more often.

. . . But remember that we are human

We are what we eat, but "food for the soul" is important, too! Healthy eating does not mean eating only the most nutritious foods. We eat certain foods depending on how we feel, what traditions we have, what our friends serve us, and of course, what we simply enjoy. In planning what to eat, it is important to balance all those aspects in order to have a healthy diet that we can eat throughout life. Variety is the spice of life—there is nothing you must never eat. Make nutrition the basis of your usual diet, and then add the extras in small amounts to ensure a healthy enjoyable diet for life. Enjoy a cozy meal at your favourite restaurant, celebrate the holiday season with traditional fare, or share an evening of food and fun with good friends—just keep it in balance.

How to use this book for healthy balanced eating

There are many vegetarian recipes throughout the book. These are marked with ✳ for easy identification, in the sections on Appetizers, Soups, Brunches and Light Meals, Pastas and Grains, and Main Courses.

To help you sort out the information that may be important for you from each of the recipes, we have highlighted some key points for most of the recipes in this cookbook.

Nutrition notes: Power-packed foods can be incorporated into all kinds of tasty recipes. Nutrition notes are provided to help you include those heart-healthy nutrients in the meals you eat each day. Nutrition notes also alert you to food components that need to be eaten only in small amounts to keep your diet in balance.

Nutritional analysis: Numbers can give you a pretty good idea of how your diet sizes up in relation to your fat budget and other daily recommended intakes. The nutritional analysis includes the amount of calories, protein, fat, saturated fat, carbohydrate, cholesterol, sodium and fibre in a portion of the recipe. Tally up the numbers, if you like, to see how your diet rates. When salt in the recipe is included as "salt to taste," sodium content of the salt has not been included in the analysis. Nutritional analysis was done using Nutritionist IV Diet analysis software 4.1™.

Timesaver tips: Although recipes are best prepared as described, there are days when time just doesn't allow for any frills in food preparation. Timesaver tips are included where possible, as an option for those busy days when every minute counts.

Just a note . . .

The recipes and comments in this cookbook are intended for use by healthy individuals who are trying to eat well and reduce their risk of heart disease. If your doctor or dietitian has advised you to make specific dietary changes, it is important that you continue to follow his or her advice.

appetizers

baba ghanoush

Nutrition notes:
Tahini is a thick paste made of ground sesame seeds. It is high in fat, but just a small amount gives plenty of flavour.

Nutritional analysis per 2 Tbsp (30 mL):
18 calories
1 g protein
1 g fat
0 g saturated fat
4 g carbohydrate
0 mg cholesterol
79 mg sodium
1 g fibre

Serve this dip with baked pita wedges or as a spread on sandwiches.

1	medium eggplant	1
4 Tbsp	freshly squeezed lemon juice	60 mL
1 Tbsp	tahini (sesame paste)	15 mL
1	clove garlic, minced	1
¼ tsp	salt	1.2 mL

Preheat oven to 375°F (190°C).

Pierce eggplant with a fork. Place on baking sheet and bake for about 45 minutes or until eggplant is soft. When cool enough to handle, remove skin.

Place eggplant in food processor and process until smooth. Add lemon juice, tahini, garlic and salt and process until puréed.

Makes 1 cup (240 mL).

Timesaver tip:
If you are rushed for time, microwave the eggplant on high for 10 minutes or until soft. Make sure to pierce the eggplant with a fork before microwaving to allow the steam to escape.

chickpea black bean hummus

Nutrition notes:
Beans are a good source of protein, iron, phosphorus, calcium and folic acid. Folic acid is a B vitamin that may help to reduce homocysteine levels in the blood. High levels of homocysteine have been identified as a risk factor for heart disease. The high-protein and low-fat content of beans make them an excellent choice as a meat alternative.

Nutritional analysis per 2 Tbsp (30 mL):
34 calories
2 g protein
0 g fat
0 g saturated fat
7 g carbohydrate
0 mg cholesterol
144 mg sodium
2 g fibre

Mixing different beans for hummus gives an interesting flavour and texture. Serve this spread with pita bread, pita crisps or vegetable crudités.

2	cloves garlic	2
1 tsp	ground cumin	5 mL
2 cups	canned black beans, rinsed	475 mL
1 cup	canned chickpeas, rinsed	240 mL
2 Tbsp	tahini	30 mL
	juice of $^1/_2$ lemon	
$^1/_3$ cup	water	80 mL
	salt and ground black pepper to taste	

In food processor, process garlic and cumin until garlic is crushed. Add black beans, chickpeas, tahini, lemon juice and water. Purée until smooth. Add additional lemon juice, salt and pepper to taste.

Makes $2^1/_2$ cups (600 mL).

Timesaver tip:
For a quick, balanced meal, make a wrap with a flour tortilla, hummus, fresh vegetables and a little low-fat grated cheese.

smoked salmon dip

Nutritional analysis per 2 Tbsp (30 mL):
28 calories
4 g protein
1 g fat
0 g saturated fat
1 g carbohydrate
5 mg cholesterol
123 mg sodium
0 g fibre

Use either lox or dry-smoked salmon for this smoky dip. Serve with thinly sliced baguette or crackers.

1 cup	low-fat ricotta cheese	240 mL
2 oz	smoked salmon	57 g
3 Tbsp	chopped fresh dill	45 mL
2 Tbsp	capers, rinsed	30 mL
1 Tbsp	lemon juice	15 mL
1 Tbsp	horseradish	15 mL

Process ricotta until smooth in food processor. Add salmon, dill, capers, lemon juice and horseradish. Process until blended.

Makes 1^1/$_2$ cups (360 mL).

Timesaver tip:
Buy smoked salmon low-fat cream cheese. Add your own herbs and blend thoroughly for a fresh homemade touch.

sun-dried tomato pâté

Nutrition notes:
White kidney beans are also known as cannellini beans. They are just as flavourful and high in fibre as the red variety.

Nutritional analysis per 2 Tbsp (30 mL):
50 calories
3 g protein
1 g fat
0 g saturated fat
9 g carbohydrate
0 mg cholesterol
295 mg sodium
3 g fibre

Use this thick, rich tomato spread on sandwiches instead of mayonnaise, or as a dip with pita bread and sliced vegetables.

2 cups	sun-dried tomatoes (not oil-packed)	475 mL
2	cloves garlic, crushed	2
1/4 cup	fresh basil leaves	60 mL
2 tsp	olive oil	10 mL
1/4 tsp	salt	1.2 mL
1/4 tsp	ground black pepper	1.2 mL
1	19-oz (540-mL) can white kidney beans, drained and rinsed	1

Soak sun-dried tomatoes in boiling water for 10 minutes. Drain tomatoes and reserve liquid. Combine all ingredients in food processor and process until smooth. Add some of reserved tomato liquid if consistency is too thick.

Makes about 2 cups (475 mL).

Timesaver tip:
For a quick appetizer, buy flavoured hummus or antipasto and serve with crackers and pita crisps.

artichoke pesto dip

Nutrition notes:
Artichoke hearts canned in water contain almost no fat, but those marinated in oil contain 11 grams of fat in just ¹/4 cup (60 mL). Fresh artichokes might seem cumbersome to prepare and eat, but they are a real treat and easier than you might think. First trim the outer leaves, then steam the artichoke. When cooked, remove each leaf and pull the lower part through your teeth. When you get to the heart, cut away the choke and enjoy the tender, most choice part of the artichoke.

Nutritional analysis per 2 Tbsp (30 mL):
52 calories
3 g protein
2 g fat
1 g saturated fat
5 g carbohydrate
3 mg cholesterol
174 mg sodium
0 g fibre

Serve this pesto dip with warm pita bread, grilled vegetables, olives and low-fat goat cheese, all arranged on a large platter.

1 Tbsp	olive oil	15 mL
¹/4	onion, chopped	¹/4
1	19-oz (540-mL) can water-packed artichoke hearts, drained and quartered	1
4	cloves garlic, crushed	4
1	4-in (10-cm) sprig fresh rosemary	1
1	2-in (5-cm) sprig fresh thyme	1
	juice of ¹/2 lemon	
	rind of ¹/2 lemon, in large strips	
1 cup	loosely packed fresh basil leaves	240 mL
¹/4 cup	grated Romano cheese	60 mL
¹/4 cup	plain non-fat yogurt	60 mL

Place oil in non-stick frying pan. Sauté onions, artichokes, garlic, rosemary, thyme, lemon juice and lemon rind for 5 minutes. Remove rosemary, thyme and lemon rind. Put sautéed ingredients, basil, Romano cheese and yogurt in food processor and process until smooth.

Makes about 1¹/4 cups (300 mL).

Timesaver tip:
Make this a day ahead—it's even more delicious the next day.

black bean dip

Nutrition notes:
Creamy dips are usually high in saturated fats; "red" dips, such as salsa and other tomato- or pepper-based types, usually contain much less fat.

Nutritional analysis per 2 Tbsp (30 mL):
25 calories
2 g protein
0 g fat
0 g saturated fat
5 g carbohydrate
0 mg cholesterol
142 mg sodium
1 g fibre

Serve this dip with herbed pita crisps or as a base for vegetable wraps. Look for pickled sliced jalapeños with other pickles or in the Mexican section of most supermarkets.

1	19-oz (540-mL) can black beans, rinsed and drained	1
2	cloves garlic	2
$^1/_4$ cup	coarsely chopped red onion	60 mL
5	slices pickled jalapeños	5
1 Tbsp	jalapeño juice	15 mL
$^3/_4$ cup	fat-free sour cream	180 mL
$^1/_2$ tsp	ground cumin	2.5 mL
$^1/_4$ tsp	salt	1.2 mL
	dash ground black pepper	

Place all ingredients in food processor. Blend until smooth.

Makes about 2$^3/_4$ cups (650 mL).

Timesaver tip:
Simple dips can be made using store-bought dips as a base. Add chopped ripe avocado to a small jar of tomato, black bean and corn salsa for a simple dip. Although high in fat, small amounts of avocado can be a tasty addition to a fat-reduced diet.

crab and cream cheese dip

Nutrition notes:
Not only are shellfish low in fat, they are also low in calories: 3 ounces (85 g) of cooked crabmeat contributes only 85 calories and 1 gram of fat, yet provides almost $^{1}/_{3}$ of an average person's protein needs for one day.

Nutritional analysis per 2 Tbsp (30 mL):
28 calories
5 g protein
0 g fat
0 g saturated fat
1 g carbohydrate
8 mg cholesterol
148 mg sodium
0 g fibre

Serve this super easy dip with sesame crackers or sliced baguettes.

8 oz	ultra light cream cheese	225 g
1 Tbsp	skim milk	15 mL
2 tsp	Worcestershire sauce	10 mL
4 oz	canned crabmeat	113 g
2 Tbsp	chopped green onions	30 mL

Preheat oven to 350°F (175°C).

In small bowl, cream together cream cheese, milk and Worcestershire sauce until smooth. Add remaining ingredients and mix well. Put into small ovenproof serving dish. Bake uncovered for 20 minutes, or until mixture is bubbly. Let sit 10 minutes before serving.

Makes about 1$^{1}/_{2}$ cups (360 mL).

herbed pita crisps

Nutrition notes:
Lighten up appetizers for an overall healthy diet. Traditional appetizers, such as mini-quiches, sausage rolls and regular chips with dip, add unwanted extra calories and fat, especially when there is dinner yet to come. Instead, try appetizers such as sushi rolls, bean and vegetable dips, bruschettas, broiled seafood or fresh fruit platters.

Nutritional analysis per 2 wedges:
22 calories
1 g protein
1 g fat
0 g saturated fat
3 g carbohydrate
1 mg cholesterol
86 mg sodium
0 g fibre

Serve these pita crisps as is, or with a dip. Vary the toppings—use different types of herbs, such as rosemary or basil, and try a variety of cheeses, such as grated light Cheddar or light mozzarella. Omit the Parmesan cheese if you are using the crisps for a cheesy dip.

3	pita breads	3
	oil spray	
1/4 tsp	salt	1.2 mL
1/4 tsp	ground black pepper	1.2 mL
2 Tbsp	light Parmesan cheese	30 mL
1 tsp	dried oregano	5 mL

Preheat oven to 375°F (190°C).

Split pita breads into halves by cutting along the outside edge of the pita round. Spray the inside of each round with oil spray. Cut each single round into 8 wedges. Set aside.

Place salt, pepper, Parmesan cheese and oregano in large plastic bag. Shake to combine the ingredients. Place pita wedges into bag, 12 pieces at a time and shake until the oiled side of each wedge is coated. Arrange wedges, coated side up, on baking sheets. Bake for about 5–8 minutes, or until pita wedges are golden and crisp.

Makes 24 wedges.

Timesaver tip:
Using oil spray from a spritzer saves time, mess and excess fat.

papaya and cheese quesadillas

Nutrition notes:
It is the fat in milk products that is high in cholesterol-raising saturated fats. The non-fat part of dairy products is an excellent source of protein and calcium, which are essential nutrients for maintaining health. So look for low-fat or fat-free versions of your favourite milk products and include them daily as part of a healthy diet.

Nutritional analysis per piece:
98 calories
3 g protein
4 g fat
1 g saturated fat
13 g carbohydrate
6 mg cholesterol
129 mg sodium
1 g fibre

The smooth sweet flavour of papaya and Brie melted together, along with the zip of jalapeño, make these a wonderful taste sensation. Use low-fat mozzarella cheese if low-fat Brie is not available.

$1/2$	white onion, thinly sliced	$1/2$
6	6-in (15-cm) flour tortillas	6
1	papaya, peeled, seeded and sliced	1
1	red bell pepper, thinly sliced	1
1	jalapeño pepper, thinly sliced	1
3 oz	low-fat Brie cheese, sliced	85 g
1 tsp	oil	5 mL

Place sliced onion in small bowl and cover with boiling water. Let sit for 5 minutes and drain.

On one half of each tortilla, sprinkle onions, papaya and peppers. Top with cheese. Fold each tortilla in half to cover filling. Lightly grease or spray large non-stick frying pan or griddle with oil.

Grill for 4 minutes on each side, until tortilla is lightly browned on both sides and cheese is melted. Cut each quesadilla in half and arrange on serving plate.

Makes 12 pieces.

Timesaver tip:
Arrange prepared quesadillas on a baking sheet. Cover with foil and bake in 375°F (190°C) oven until cheese is melted and quesadillas are hot.

bean bruschetta

**Nutritional analysis
per bruschetta:**
35 calories
2 g protein
0 g fat
0 g saturated fat
7 g carbohydrate
0 mg cholesterol
111 mg sodium
1 g fibre

Mixing the beans with fresh basil and lemon juice gives this spread a light yet refreshing taste. To roast red bell peppers: place whole pepper on baking sheet and bake at 375°F (190°C) for 45 minutes, or until skin is blistered and slightly darkened. Peel skin off when slightly cooled.

1	19-oz (540-mL) can white kidney beans, drained and rinsed	1
1/4 cup	chopped fresh basil	60 mL
1 Tbsp	lemon juice	15 mL
1	clove garlic, crushed	1
1 Tbsp	tomato paste	15 mL
25	thin slices baguette, toasted	25
1	roasted red bell pepper, thinly sliced	1

Preheat oven to 425°F (220°C).

Purée beans, basil, lemon juice, garlic and tomato paste. Spread each baguette slice with 1 Tbsp (15 mL) bean purée and top with pepper slice. Bake until heated through.

Makes 25 bruschetta.

dolmathes

**Nutritional analysis
per roll:**
21 calories
1 g protein
1 g fat
0 g saturated fat
2 g carbohydrate
0 mg cholesterol
52 mg sodium
0 g fibre

Everyone who makes dolmathes has their own secret for success. Some experts say that the dab of tomato paste is the key, while others insist it is the addition of pine nuts that makes the dish. Serve with lemon wedges and plain yogurt.

1	2-lb (900-g) jar grape leaves	1
2 Tbsp	olive oil	30 mL
1	bunch green onions, finely chopped	1
2 Tbsp	finely chopped parsley	30 mL
2 Tbsp	finely chopped dill	30 mL
³/₄ cup	long-grain rice	180 mL
2 Tbsp	pine nuts	30 mL
1 tsp	tomato paste	5 mL
¹/₄ cup	dry white wine	60 mL
¹/₄ tsp	salt	1.2 mL
¹/₄ tsp	ground black pepper	1.2 mL
	juice of 2 lemons	
1	10-oz (284-mL) can beef bouillon or chicken broth	1
1 cup	water	240 mL

Remove grape leaves from jar. Rinse leaves with hot water and drain. If any leaves have stems, cut off stems. Pat each leaf dry and place, shiny side down, on paper towels. Set aside any leaves that are torn or appear excessively large and tough.

Heat oil in medium saucepan over medium heat. Add onions and sauté until softened. Add parsley, dill, rice, pine nuts, tomato paste, wine, salt and pepper. Sauté for 2 minutes or until wine is almost evaporated. Place rice mixture into bowl and let cool. Rinse saucepan and line bottom with damaged leaves.

Place 1 tsp (5 mL) of cooled rice mixture in centre of each undamaged leaf. Fold bottom of leaf up over rice mixture. Fold in sides and then roll up carefully into a cylinder. Take care not to roll dolmathes too tightly, as rice will expand when cooked.

Arrange dolmathes in bottom of prepared saucepan, sprinkling each layer with lemon juice. Pour bouillon and water into pot. Place dinner plate on top of dolmathes to weight them down. Cover pot with lid. Bring to a boil and then simmer over low heat for 50 minutes. Drain and let cool.

Makes 40 dolmathes.

Note: If you have grapevines, it is well worth the effort to pick your own leaves. Pick them in spring when they are small and tender. Blanch the leaves in small batches until they change colour, approximately 15 seconds. Blanched grape leaves will keep in the fridge for 2 days, or freeze them flat in small batches in plastic freezer bags. Frozen grape leaves should keep in a chest freezer for up to 6 months.

Timesaver tip:
Store-bought dolmathes are delicious. Buy the vegetarian ones stuffed with rice instead of meat. Make sure you pat off any excess oil before eating them.

teriyaki chicken brochettes

Nutrition notes:
Remove skin from chicken before cooking if chicken will be cooked in a sauce. However, if you are barbecuing or roasting chicken, the skin can be removed after cooking.

Nutritional analysis per skewer:
94 calories
14 g protein
1 g fat
0 g saturated fat
6 g carbohydrate
33 mg cholesterol
165 mg sodium
0 g fibre

Chicken on skewers is a tasty, low-fat alternative to serving chicken wings as appetizers. Make the kebabs ahead of time, and pop the skewers of chicken in the oven just before serving.

4	boneless, skinless chicken breast halves	4
³/₄ cup	water	180 mL
2 Tbsp	light soy sauce	30 mL
2 Tbsp	brown sugar	30 mL
1 Tbsp	sweet wine	15 mL
1	clove garlic, crushed	1
1	1-in (2.5-cm) piece fresh ginger, peeled and sliced	1
2 Tbsp	cornstarch	30 mL
2 Tbsp	cold water	30 mL
2 tsp	sesame seeds	10 mL

Preheat oven to 375°F (190°C). Soak eight 6-in (15-cm) bamboo skewers in water for 30 minutes before using.

Cut chicken breast into 1-in (2.5-cm) cubes. In medium pot, combine ³/₄ cup (180 mL) water, soy sauce, sugar, wine, garlic and ginger. Add chicken pieces. Bring to boil over medium heat. Simmer for 5 minutes, or until chicken pieces are just cooked. Remove chicken from pot, saving liquid in pot.

Combine cornstarch with 2 Tbsp (30 mL) water and mix well. Add to liquid in pot. Bring liquid to a boil over medium heat, stirring constantly until thickened. Set aside.

Thread 3–4 pieces of chicken onto each bamboo skewer. Put in baking pan in single layer. Pour sauce over chicken pieces (not over skewer ends). Sprinkle with sesame seeds. Bake in oven for 15 minutes, or until sauce is sizzling and chicken is hot.

Makes 8 skewers.

Timesaver tip:
For a main course, make teriyaki chicken pieces instead of chicken on skewers. Remove skin from chicken pieces and cook chicken in sauce as indicated above. Remove chicken from liquid and place in shallow baking dish. Thicken sauce with cornstarch as above, and pour over chicken. Bake uncovered in 375°F (190°C) oven until sauce is bubbly. Tastes great using skinless chicken thighs and drumsticks, too!

phyllo triangles with pear and pecans

Nutrition notes:
Use your imagination to keep snacks interesting. Instead of high-fat cookies and bars, make low-fat versions of these traditional goodies to enhance the variety and zest of a healthy diet. Use phyllo pastry with a touch of oil to replace the pastries and crusts used in turnovers and tarts.

Nutritional analysis per triangle:
48 calories
2 g protein
2 g fat
0 g saturated fat
7 g carbohydrate
0 mg cholesterol
104 mg sodium
0 g fibre

Fat-free cheese slices add almost no saturated fat to this delectable appetizer. But if you still have room in your daily fat budget, try low-fat Brie instead.

1	large Bosc pear, peeled, quartered and cored	1
1/4 cup	coarsely chopped pecans	60 mL
1/4 cup	apricot jam	60 mL
1 Tbsp	orange liqueur	15 mL
6	slices fat-free processed Swiss cheese	6
6	sheets phyllo pastry oil spray	6

Preheat oven to 375°F (190°C). Cut each quarter pear crosswise into 1/4-in (.6-cm) slices to make pieces that are approximately 1 in (2.5 cm) long and 1/4 in (.6 cm) thick. Set aside. In small bowl, combine pecans, jam and liqueur. Set aside. Cut each slice of cheese into 4 quarters. Set aside.

Cut each phyllo sheet into 4 pieces lengthwise (sheets are easier to cut while rolled up). Place one phyllo strip on your work surface. Spray lightly with oil. Place one piece of pear on bottom corner of phyllo. Top with about 1 tsp (5 mL) pecan mixture. Top with cheese quarter. Cover filling by folding phyllo over the filling, making a triangle at the bottom edge. Continue to fold in triangles along the length of the phyllo. The completed triangle should be about 2½ x 3½ in (6 x 9 cm). Repeat with each phyllo piece to make 24 triangles. Place triangles on non-stick baking sheet and bake for 10–15 minutes, or until pear is hot and phyllo is golden. Serve hot.

Makes 24 triangles.

soups

carrot soup

Nutrition notes:
Everyone associates carrots with vitamin A and healthy eyes. But carrots are also loaded with other nutrients, such as potassium, vitamin C, folic acid and magnesium.

Nutritional analysis per serving:
142 calories
6 g protein
4 g fat
1 g saturated fat
21 g carbohydrate
0 mg cholesterol
879 mg sodium
3 g fibre

"Beta-carotene soup" could be another name for this soup that's loaded with carrots and yams! So nutritious, a little different, yet it uses everyday ingredients that you have in your house.

1	medium yam	1
1	large potato	1
6	carrots, peeled and sliced	6
1 Tbsp	oil	15 mL
1	onion, chopped	1
5 cups	chicken broth	1.2 L
1/4 tsp	salt	1.2 mL
1/4 tsp	ground black pepper	1.2 mL
1 Tbsp	lemon juice	15 ml

Preheat oven to 400°F (200°C). Cut yam and potato into quarters and wrap in foil. Place on baking sheet and bake until soft, about 45 minutes. Let cool.

Cook carrots in boiling water until tender. Heat oil in large pot over medium heat. Add onions and sauté until golden. Place onions and cooked carrots in food processor. Deglaze pot with a little chicken broth and add to food processor. Purée. Peel potato and yam. Add potato, yam, salt, pepper and lemon juice to food processor and purée until smooth.

Pour mixture back into pot. Add remaining chicken stock. Simmer over low heat for 15 minutes.

Serves 6.

Timesaver tip:
Sauté onions, then add remaining vegetables, spices and chicken broth. Cook until vegetables are soft. Purée. Return to pot, add lemon juice and heat through.

salmon chowder

Nutrition notes:
A cream soup made with skim milk is an excellent source of calcium without the saturated fat found in dairy fats. Use the skimmed version whenever a recipe calls for any dairy product.

Nutritional analysis per serving:
177 calories
14 g protein
4 g fat
1 g saturated fat
23 g carbohydrate
20 mg cholesterol
280 mg sodium
2 g fibre

Other fish, such as red snapper, can be used instead of salmon for a subtler fish flavour. Add a can of crabmeat to make a more substantial soup.

1 Tbsp	margarine	15 mL
1 cup	chopped celery	240 mL
1 cup	chopped onion	240 mL
2 cups	potatoes, peeled and diced into $1/2$-in (1.2-cm) cubes	475 mL
$1/2$ cup	flour	120 mL
$1/4$ tsp	ground black pepper	1.2 mL
1 tsp	salt	5 mL
1 Tbsp	dried parsley flakes	15 mL
5 cups	skim milk	1.2 L
2 cups	salmon, cut into 1-in (2.5-cm) cubes	475 mL

Melt margarine in large non-stick pot. Add celery, onion and potatoes and sauté over low heat for 20 minutes, stirring often to prevent browning or sticking. Vegetables should be just partially cooked.

Mix together flour, pepper, salt and parsley. Stir into partially cooked vegetables. Slowly add milk, cooking and stirring until soup thickens. Add salmon. Cook until salmon is just done, about 5 minutes. The flesh will be opaque when cooked. Adjust seasoning with salt and pepper.

Serves 8.

Timesaver tip:
If fresh salmon isn't available, or you just want to save preparation and cleanup time, use two $7^1/2$-oz (213-g) cans of salmon broken into small chunks.

salmon and vegetable soup

Nutrition notes:
Cream-style corn is not fatty as the name implies—it's simply creamy in texture and flavour. The bonus is that corn is one vegetable especially high in phytosterols.

Nutritional analysis per serving:
236 calories
14 g protein
5 g fat
1 g saturated fat
36 g carbohydrate
11 mg cholesterol
651 mg sodium
4 g fibre

This main-course soup is really a vegetable and corn chowder with a taste of salmon. Team it up with warm rolls and baby greens tossed with honey lemon dressing for a quick dinner.

2 tsp	oil	10 mL
$^1/_2$ cup	chopped celery	120 mL
$^1/_2$ cup	chopped onion	120 mL
$^1/_4$ cup	chopped green bell pepper	60 mL
1	clove garlic, minced	1
3 cups	potato, diced	720 mL
1 cup	carrots, sliced	240 mL
1 cup	chicken broth	240 mL
1 cup	water	240 mL
1 cup	zucchini, sliced thinly	240 mL
1	7 $^1/_2$-oz (213-g) can pink salmon, with liquid	1
1	13$^1/_2$-oz (385-mL) can evaporated skim milk	1
1	14-oz (398-mL) can cream-style corn	1
$^1/_4$ cup	chopped fresh parsley	60 mL
1 tsp	chopped fresh dill	5 mL
$^1/_4$ tsp	ground black pepper	1.2 mL

Heat oil in large pot over medium heat. Add celery, onion, green pepper and garlic. Sauté until softened, but not browned.

Add potatoes, carrots, chicken broth and water. Bring to a boil. Simmer for 15 minutes, or until potatoes and carrots are cooked. Add zucchini and cook for 5 more minutes.

Break apart salmon and crush bones. Add salmon and liquid, evaporated milk, corn, parsley, dill and pepper to vegetables in pot. Heat slowly, stirring often, until soup is bubbly and hot.

Serves 6.

Timesaver tip:
It may seem that there are too many ingredients in this recipe for quick preparation, but it is just the vegetables that need a lot of chopping. Use the food processor to chop vegetables when the recipe calls for much chopping and slicing, especially in soups where the final shape of the vegetables is not crucial. It's worth taking the time to slice or dice vegetables manually when the size and shape of the vegetables will enhance the eye-appeal, such as in a stir-fry.

chicken corn soup

Nutrition notes:
Bouillon cubes and
regular canned chicken
broth are high in sodium.
If you need to limit your
sodium intake, use
homemade chicken
broth, or buy canned
low-sodium varieties.

**Nutritional analysis
per serving:**
130 calories
10 g protein
1 g fat
0 g saturated fat
22 g carbohydrate
17 mg cholesterol
590 mg sodium
1 g fibre

Team this homey-tasting soup with a main-course salad, such as Rice and Bean Salad (page 94) for a weekend lunch. For an Asian flavour, add 1 tsp (5 mL) sesame oil just before serving.

1	skinless chicken breast half	1
4 cups	water	950 mL
1	chicken bouillon cube	1
1	14-oz (398-mL) can cream-style corn	1
¹/₈ tsp	ground black pepper	.5 mL
¹/₄ cup	egg whites, or 2 egg whites	60 mL
2 Tbsp	cornstarch	30 mL
¹/₄ cup	cold water	60 mL

Simmer chicken breast in at least 4 cups (950 mL) water until cooked, about 15 minutes. Remove chicken from pot, reserving broth. Remove chicken meat from bone. Dice chicken and set aside.

Skim fat off broth. Return 3 cups (720 mL) of chicken broth to pot and bring to a boil. Add bouillon cube and mix until dissolved. Add corn, chicken and pepper. Return to a boil. Reduce heat to medium-low, and while stirring, add egg whites. Mix together cornstarch and ¹/₄ cup (60 mL) cold water. Add to corn mixture while stirring. Continue to stir until soup is thickened.

Serves 4.

Timesaver tip:
Use ¹/₂ cup (120 mL) cooked diced chicken instead of chicken breast. Add to 3 cups (720 mL) of boiling water. Continue with rest of recipe.

tomato lentil soup

Nutrition notes:
Lentils are one of those power-packed foods that give us so much nutrition in just one portion. Not only are they a great source of protein and fibre, they are one of the highest food sources of folic acid. Just one cup of cooked lentils contains 15 grams of fibre, 18 grams of protein and 350 micrograms of folic acid.

Nutritional analysis per serving:
179 calories
12 g protein
1 g fat
0 g saturated fat
31 g carbohydrate
1 mg cholesterol
530 mg sodium
12 g fibre

So thick, it could be called a stew. Use any vegetables you have on hand, such as zucchini, broccoli and green beans. Soups laden with all kinds of vegetables are a great way to include vegetables in the diet, especially for those cold days when salads may not seem so enticing.

2	10-oz (284-mL) cans chicken broth	2
2^1/$_2$ cups	water	600 mL
2 cups	dried green lentils	475 mL
1	medium onion	1
2	medium carrots, peeled	2
2	stalks celery	2
1	green bell pepper, seeded	1
1	red bell pepper, seeded	1
2	potatoes, peeled and diced	2
1	28-oz (796-mL) can diced tomatoes	1
1	14-oz (398-mL) can stewed tomatoes	1
1 tsp	curry powder	5 mL

Place chicken broth and water in large pot. Rinse lentils in cold water, drain and add to pot. Finely chop onion, carrots, celery and peppers. Add to pot and cover. Bring mixture to a boil, lower heat and simmer covered for 45 minutes, until lentils are tender. Add potatoes, diced and stewed tomatoes, and curry powder. Return to a boil, and simmer for 30 minutes longer.

Serves 12.

Timesaver tip:
Add canned lentils and extra vegetables to canned vegetable soup.

vegetarian borscht

Nutrition notes:
You can tell there are plenty of flavonoids in beets because of their deep red colour. Add grated fresh beets to salads, use roasted or boiled beets as a side vegetable, or marinate cooked beets in a vinaigrette dressing to boost your flavonoid intake.

Nutritional analysis per serving:
110 calories
5 g protein
0 g fat
0 g saturated fat
23 g carbohydrate
0 mg cholesterol
399 mg sodium
5 g fibre

This soup is full of vegetables that fight heart disease—cabbage, chard and beets. Serve with crusty bread and a salad for a light summer meal.

12	small beets, washed and halved	12
8 cups	water	2 L
2	medium carrots, peeled and sliced into rounds	2
2 cups	sliced savoy cabbage	475 mL
1 cup	finely sliced Swiss chard	240 mL
4	cloves garlic, minced	4
2	bay leaves	2
1	28-oz (796-mL) can tomatoes, roughly chopped	1
2 Tbsp	apple cider vinegar	30 mL
	juice of 1 lemon	
	salt and ground black pepper to taste	
1	bunch fresh dill, chopped	1
6 Tbsp	low-fat plain yogurt	90 mL

In large soup pot, cook beets in water until tender. Drain beets, reserving liquid, and let cool. Hold beets under running water and remove skins.

Grate beets and put them back into soup pot. Add reserved cooking liquid, carrots, cabbage, Swiss chard, garlic, bay leaves and canned tomatoes. Bring to a boil. Reduce heat to simmer and cook, covered, for 1 hour. Season with cider vinegar, lemon juice, salt and pepper. Add extra water if soup is too thick. Before serving add chopped dill. Top each serving with dollop of yogurt.

Serves 6.

creamy cauliflower soup

Nutrition notes:
To lighten up cream soups, use skim milk, evaporated skim milk or fat-free soy milk instead of cream or whole milk. Add a slurry of flour and water or purée some of the vegetables to thicken the soup, rather than using a roux (butter and flour mixture).

Nutritional analysis per serving:
192 calories
9 g protein
5 g fat
1 g saturated fat
30 g carbohydrate
4 mg cholesterol
556 mg sodium
5 g fibre

To add a touch of sweetness to the soup, use a yam instead of a carrot. Serve with Herbed Pita Crisps (page 25) and a bean dip.

3^1/$_2$ cups	cauliflower florets	840 mL
2 cups	skim milk	475 mL
1 Tbsp	oil	15 mL
^{1}/$_2$	onion, diced	^{1}/$_2$
1	potato, peeled and diced	1
1	carrot, diced	1
1	10-oz (284-mL) can chicken broth	1
1^1/$_4$ cups	water	300 mL
	ground black pepper to taste	

In saucepan, cook cauliflower in milk until soft, about 10 minutes. Drain cauliflower, reserve milk and set aside.

Heat oil over medium heat in large soup pot. Add onions and sauté for 5 minutes. Add potato and carrots. Cook for 2 minutes. Add chicken broth and water and simmer until vegetables are fork-tender. Add cauliflower. Purée with hand blender or food processor. Return to soup pot. Add reserved milk. Season with pepper. Add additional milk if desired. Heat through.

Serves 4.

harvest corn chowder

Nutrition notes:
Corn, although considered a vegetable, is actually a grain. Make sure you include plenty of other vegetables when eating corn.

Nutritional analysis per serving:
227 calories
10 g protein
4 g fat
1 g saturated fat
41 g carbohydrate
2 mg cholesterol
819 mg sodium
4 g fibre

For a true harvest chowder, make this in the fall when fresh corn is available. Roast the corn in the oven or over the barbecue, remove the kernels, and add them to the soup instead of frozen kernels.

1 Tbsp	olive oil	15 mL
1 cup	chopped onion	240 mL
	dash hot pepper flakes	
2 cups	potatoes, peeled and diced	475 mL
$^1/_2$ cup	chopped celery	120 mL
$^1/_2$ cup	diced carrot	120 mL
$^1/_2$ cup	chopped red bell pepper	120 mL
2	10-oz (284-mL) cans chicken broth	2
$3^3/_4$ cups	water	900 mL
2 cups	frozen corn kernels	475 mL
1	14-oz (398-mL) can cream-style corn	1
$1^1/_2$ cups	skim milk	360 mL
2 Tbsp	chopped cilantro (optional)	30 mL
	salt and ground black pepper to taste	

Heat oil in large saucepan over high heat. Add onion and pepper flakes, reduce heat to medium and sauté for 2 minutes. Add potatoes, celery, carrot and red pepper. Cook for 2 minutes. Add chicken broth and water. Bring to a boil.

Reduce heat and cook for 10 minutes, or until vegetables are tender-crisp. Add corn kernels, creamed corn and milk. Cook until heated through. Stir in cilantro, if desired. Season with salt and pepper.

Serves 6.

butternut squash soup

Nutrition notes:
Butternut squash is rich in vitamin C and beta-carotene. In fact, most squashes, including pumpkin, are high in these antioxidant vitamins. Puréed squash can be added to any soups, or even mashed potatoes, to boost the nutrition content.

Nutritional analysis per serving:
141 calories
4 g protein
2 g fat
0 g saturated fat
25 g carbohydrate
0 mg cholesterol
411 mg sodium
3 g fibre

The swirl of yogurt mellows out the powerful flavour of the spices. MacIntosh apples are best in this soup, but any apples will work.

2 tsp	oil	10 mL
1	large onion, chopped	1
2	cloves garlic, minced	2
3	apples, peeled, cored and chopped	3
1 Tbsp	minced fresh ginger	15 mL
1 Tbsp	curry powder	15 mL
1/2 tsp	ground cumin	2.5 mL
6 cups	peeled, seeded and cubed butternut squash (2 lbs/900 g)	1.5 L
4 cups	chicken broth	950 mL
1 cup	apple juice	240 mL
	salt and ground black pepper to taste	
1/2 cup	non-fat plain yogurt (optional)	120 mL

Heat oil in large soup pot over medium heat. Add onion and sauté until softened. Add garlic and apples, and sauté until apples are soft. Add ginger, curry powder and cumin, and cook for 2 minutes. Add squash, chicken broth and apple juice. Bring to a boil. Reduce heat and simmer for 30–40 minutes, or until squash is tender.

Strain soup mixture and reserve liquid. Purée solids in food processor or with hand blender until smooth. Return liquid and puréed mixture to soup pot. Heat through. Season with salt and pepper, and adjust spices. Add a dollop of yogurt to each bowl before serving, if desired.

Serves 8.

miso vegetable soup

Nutrition notes:
Miso and dashi soup
bases are high in sodium
and should be used
sparingly.

**Nutritional analysis
per serving:**
89 calories
7 g protein
4 g fat
1 g saturated fat
8 g carbohydrate
0 mg cholesterol
721 mg sodium
2 g fibre

Sui choi is an Oriental cabbage that has a milder flavour and more tender leaves than regular cabbage. Using any leafy vegetable in this soup, though, will complement the miso flavour. Dashi is a soup base used in many Japanese dishes. Miso and dashi are available at most supermarkets that carry Japanese food products.

4 cups	water	950 mL
1 tsp	dashi ($^1/_2$ packet)	5 mL
2 cups	greens, such as sui choi, thinly sliced cabbage or spinach leaves	475 mL
$^1/_4$ cup	miso	60 mL
$^1/_2$ lb	medium-firm tofu, cubed	225 g
1	green onion, thinly sliced	1

Bring water to a boil in medium saucepan. Add dashi. Add greens and cook until almost done, about 5 minutes. Add miso and dissolve. Add tofu and green onions. Simmer until tofu is heated through.

Serves 4.

Timesaver tip:
Instant miso soup packets can be purchased in supermarkets selling Oriental foods. Add a packet to boiling water in a pot, and add cubed tofu and greens for a quick miso vegetable soup. Add extra tofu, simulated crabmeat and vegetables to make a meal-in-a-pot.

vegetables

power-packed vegetables!

All food groups in Canada's Food Guide are essential for good health, and that includes vegetables. With everyone rushing from one meeting to another, or coming home late and having to make dinner, vegetables often get left behind. Yet this is the one group of foods that is full of vitamins, minerals, phytochemicals and fibre, but light in calories. We should be eating hefty amounts of vegetables every day. Try some of these tasty, simple ideas to help make vegetables a significant part of your diet.

- Season steamed green beans, asparagus, snow peas, or carrots with a little olive oil, lemon juice, salt and pepper.
- Roast winter vegetables, such as sliced carrots, rutabaga and parsnip, along with onions and a little margarine or oil in a roasting pan. The caramelized onions will enhance the flavour of the roasted vegetables.
- Use a "barbecue wok" to grill a combination of vegetables, such as cauliflower, broccoli, onion and red peppers. Put all cut-up vegetables in a plastic bag first, shake with a little olive oil, oregano, salt and pepper to taste, and then grill on the barbecue in the barbecue wok.
- Make barbecued vegetable kebabs by skewering vegetables, such as cut-up bell pepper, zucchini, onion and whole mushrooms. Brush with a glaze, such as teriyaki sauce, or simply spray with olive oil and barbecue.
- Spaghetti squash is an interesting quick addition to any dinner. Cut a medium-size spaghetti squash in half lengthwise and remove the seeds. Place cut side down in a glass baking dish. Add just enough water to cover the bottom of the dish. Cover loosely with plastic wrap. Microwave on high for about 7–8 minutes, or until the squash is tender. Scrape the inside of the squash crosswise with a fork to loosen the strands of squash. Add a little maple syrup and lemon juice for added flavour, if you like.

- Fresh baby vegetables make a delicious appetizer. For an interesting presentation, line a basket with foil and then kale leaves. Use whole unpeeled small carrots, steamed asparagus spears or whole green beans, cherry tomatoes and raw sugar snap peas. Baby zucchini and whole artichoke make unique additions.
- Jazz up a vegetable soup mix by adding whatever vegetables you have in the kitchen to the soup pot. Add chopped leftover chicken and pasta to make a main-course soup.
- Always add vegetables to any sandwich you make. Lettuce, tomatoes, sprouts and cucumbers are great standbys, but grilled or barbecued vegetables are also scrumptious.

cucumber shrimp salad

Nutrition notes:
Although shellfish, such as scallops and crab, are low in cholesterol, $3^1/2$ oz (100 g) of shrimp contains almost 200 mg of cholesterol. But shrimp are tasty delicacies that can be used in small amounts to enhance the flavour of healthy dishes.

Nutritional analysis per serving:
69 calories
5 g protein
1 g fat
0 g saturated fat
12 g carbohydrate
35 mg cholesterol
116 mg sodium
1 g fibre

This salad is known as "sunomono," a refreshing dish served with clear vermicelli noodles in Japanese restaurants.

1	long English cucumber	1
1 tsp	salt	5 mL
	juice of 1 lemon	
2 Tbsp	sugar	30 mL
2 Tbsp	vinegar	30 mL
$^1/_4$ cup	cooked shrimp	60 mL
1 tsp	sesame seeds	5 mL

Slice cucumber as thinly as possible and put in medium bowl. Sprinkle with salt, stir and let sit for 15 minutes, until cucumber slices are softened. Drain and squeeze out extra liquid. Add more water and rinse out all the salt. Drain and squeeze out as much of the liquid as possible. Set aside.

In small bowl, combine lemon juice, sugar and vinegar. Mix well. Add shrimp to cucumbers. Pour dressing over cucumber mixture and mix gently. Place salad in serving dish, sprinkle with sesame seeds and serve.

Serves 4.

tomato basil salad

Nutrition notes:
Vinaigrettes are a
flavourful yet healthy
way to season your salads
and vegetables. Use olive
oil with any variety of
vinegar, such as balsamic,
wine, rice or cider vinegar.
Use a ratio of 1:3 for oil
and vinegar.

**Nutritional analysis
per serving:**
51 calories
1 g protein
4 g fat
1 g saturated fat
5 g carbohydrate
0 mg cholesterol
81 mg sodium
1 g fibre

The aroma of this salad is reminiscent of a summer garden. Tomatoes and basil are a perfect match. It's best if you chill the salad before serving to let the tomatoes marinate.

2 cups	cherry tomatoes, halved	475 mL
1/4 cup	chopped fresh basil	60 mL
1 Tbsp	olive oil	15 mL
2 Tbsp	red wine vinegar	30 mL
1 Tbsp	balsamic vinegar	15 mL
1/8 tsp	salt	.5 mL
1/8 tsp	ground black pepper	.5 mL

Put tomatoes and basil in small serving dish. Set aside. Mix together oil, wine vinegar and balsamic vinegar. Pour over tomatoes. Season with salt and pepper.

Serves 4.

Timesaver tip:
Toss tomatoes and chopped basil with a low-fat commercial oil and vinegar dressing.

tomato and onion salad

Nutrition notes:
Onions contain a flavonol called quercetin that may act as an antioxidant in our bodies. Red and white onions tend to be a little milder than the regular cooking variety, and are especially suitable for recipes calling for raw onions.

Nutritional analysis per serving:
92 calories
2 g protein
4 g fat
1 g saturated fat
14 g carbohydrate
0 mg cholesterol
88 mg sodium
2 g fibre

The flavour combination of juicy beefsteak tomatoes, fresh cilantro and balsamic vinegar is even better when the salad is allowed to sit for a while before serving. To serve in a salad bowl rather than on a plate, dice the tomatoes and mix with the other vegetables. If cilantro is not your favourite herb, use crushed garlic in the dressing instead.

4	tomatoes, sliced	4
$^1/_2$	red onion, thinly sliced	$^1/_2$
1 cup	mushrooms, sliced	240 mL
2 Tbsp	chopped cilantro	30 mL
3 Tbsp	balsamic vinegar	45 mL
1 Tbsp	olive oil	15 mL
2 tsp	sugar	10 mL
$^1/_8$ tsp	salt	.5 mL

Arrange tomato slices on serving plate. Top with onions, mushrooms and cilantro. Set aside. In small jar, combine remaining ingredients. Shake well. Pour over salad. Let sit for $^1/_2$ hour before serving.

Serves 4.

Timesaver tip:
Reduce the fat content of your favourite commercial vinaigrette dressing by diluting it with rice vinegar. A touch of sugar can be added to cut the acidity, if necessary.

salad greens with oriental sesame dressing

Nutrition notes:
Sesame oil contains approximately 14% saturated fat, similar to soy and olive oils. Because of its strong nutty flavour, a little sesame oil goes a long way in a bowl of salad greens.

Nutritional analysis per serving:
97 calories
2 g protein
3 g fat
0 g saturated fat
15 g carbohydrate
0 mg cholesterol
185 mg sodium
3 g fibre

Jicama is a tuber used widely in Mexico and Central America. Its slightly sweet flavour and crisp texture are a refreshing addition to any salad or raw vegetable platter.

6 cups	mixed greens	1.5 L
$^1/_2$	white onion, thinly sliced	$^1/_2$
1 cup	jicama peeled and sliced into $^1/_4$ x 1-in (.6 x 2.5-cm) sticks	240 mL
1	10-oz (284-mL) can mandarin oranges, drained	1
3 Tbsp	rice vinegar	45 mL
1 Tbsp	soy sauce	15 mL
2 tsp	canola oil	10 mL
1 tsp	sesame oil	5 mL
1 Tbsp	sugar	15 mL
$^1/_4$ tsp	dry mustard	1.2 mL
1 Tbsp	sesame seeds	15 mL

Combine mixed greens, onion, jicama and oranges in salad bowl. Set aside. In small jar, combine remaining ingredients. Shake well. Pour over salad, toss and serve immediately.

Serves 6.

Timesaver tip:
Double the dressing recipe, omit the sesame seeds and refrigerate half for up to 2 days. Add sesame seeds to dressing just before serving.

mixed greens with maple lime dressing

Nutrition notes:
Eating handfuls of sunflower seeds will add large amounts of fat to your diet, but using just a sprinkle in a salad provides flavour and beneficial nutrients with just a touch of fat.

Nutritional analysis per serving:
106 calories
4 g protein
6 g fat
1 g saturated fat
10 g carbohydrate
0 mg cholesterol
133 mg sodium
3 g fibre

A combination of red and green leaf lettuce makes a colourful salad. If sunflower sprouts are not available at your local supermarket, soybean sprouts will also give the salad an interesting texture.

6 cups	mixed greens	1.5 L
1 cup	sunflower sprouts	240 mL
2 Tbsp	sunflower seeds	30 mL
12	cherry tomatoes, cut in half	12
1 Tbsp	olive oil	15 mL
1 Tbsp	maple syrup	15 mL
	juice of 1 lime	
1 Tbsp	Dijon mustard	15 mL
$^1/_8$ tsp	salt	.5 mL
	dash ground black pepper	

In large salad bowl, combine greens, sprouts, sunflower seeds and tomatoes. Set aside.

In small jar, combine remaining ingredients and shake well. Pour over salad just before serving. Toss and serve.

Serves 4.

Timesaver tip:
Packaged salad greens are handy for busy days. For special occasions, using a package of mixed baby greens will save time and give your salad a gourmet touch.

greek salad

Nutrition notes:
There are 7 grams of fat in just 1 oz (28 g) of feta cheese, but it's loaded with flavour. Use a small amount in a large recipe to add zest to each serving without adding much fat.

Nutritional analysis per serving:
119 calories
4 g protein
8 g fat
3 g saturated fat
10 g carbohydrate
17 mg cholesterol
298 mg sodium
3 g fibre

This salad is best in summer, when garden tomatoes and fresh oregano are available. Traditionally, this salad is dressed only with olive oil and sprinkled with oregano. The olive oil has been reduced, and lemon juice and vinegar have been added to give it a tangier taste.

1	English cucumber, cut into $^3/_4$-in (2-cm) chunks	1
4	medium tomatoes, cut in eighths	4
1	yellow bell pepper, seeded and cut in strips	1
$^1/_2$	medium purple onion, thinly sliced	$^1/_2$
4 oz	feta cheese, crumbled	113 g
12	kalamata olives	12
1 Tbsp	olive oil	15 mL
1 Tbsp	red wine vinegar	15 mL
2 Tbsp	lemon juice, fresh squeezed	30 mL
1 Tbsp	dried oregano, or 3 Tbsp (45 mL) fresh	15 mL

Mix cucumber, tomatoes, pepper and onion in salad bowl. Sprinkle cheese on top and add olives. Pour oil, vinegar and lemon juice over salad. Crumble oregano over top and toss.

Serves 6.

Timesaver tip:
Use bottled, fat-free, Italian-type dressing instead of making your own. Crumble oregano over salad before serving.

green bean and red pepper salad

Nutrition notes:
Balsamic vinegar is made from Italian grapes and aged to develop a wonderful, mellow flavour that makes it easy to cut down on the amount of fats used in cooking. A splash of balsamic vinegar is great on salad greens, roasted vegetables and even pasta.

This is a perfect dish for a summer barbecue or a potluck buffet. It's easy to double or triple the recipe for a large gathering.

1 lb	green beans, trimmed	450 g
$^1/_2$	red bell pepper, seeded and sliced into strips	$^1/_2$
2 Tbsp	red wine vinegar	30 mL
1 Tbsp	balsamic vinegar	15 mL
1 tsp	olive oil	5 mL
$^1/_2$ tsp	Dijon mustard	2.5 mL
	salt and ground black pepper to taste	

Steam green beans until tender, about 5 minutes. Place in cold water to halt the cooking process and chill. Place beans in mixing bowl with red pepper.

Place remaining ingredients in glass jar and shake. Pour dressing over vegetables. Cool before serving.

Serves 4.

Nutritional analysis per serving:
59 calories
2 g protein
2 g fat
0 g saturated fat
11 g carbohydrate
0 mg cholesterol
8 mg sodium
4 g fibre

Timesaver tip:
Add extra balsamic vinegar to commercial low-fat wine vinegar dressing and toss with the green beans and red peppers.

broccoli salad

Nutrition notes:
Broccoli is a member of the cruciferous family of vegetables that includes Brussels sprouts, cabbage and kale. Not only are they high in vitamins A and C, they contain phytochemicals that may help fight disease, such as heart disease and cancer.

Nutritional analysis per serving:
113 calories
5 g protein
4 g fat
2 g saturated fat
17 g carbohydrate
7 mg cholesterol
229 mg sodium
3 g fibre

Serve this "broccoli slaw" with barbecued chicken pieces for a simple luncheon. Add homemade whole-grain bread to round out the meal.

4 cups	broccoli, chopped	950 mL
1/4 cup	sunflower seeds	60 mL
1/2 cup	raisins	120 mL
2 oz	light feta cheese, crumbled	57 g
1/2 cup	chopped red onion	120 mL
1	8-oz (227-mL) can sliced water chestnuts, drained	1
1/2 cup	low-fat plain yogurt	120 mL
1/4 cup	fat-free mayonnaise	60 mL
1 Tbsp	lemon juice	15 mL
1 Tbsp	sugar	15 mL
1/4 tsp	salt	1.2 mL
1/4 tsp	ground black pepper	1.2 mL

Combine broccoli, sunflower seeds, raisins, feta cheese, onion and water chestnuts. Set aside.

Whisk together yogurt, mayonnaise, lemon juice, sugar, salt and pepper. Add to salad mixture and mix well.

Serves 8.

Timesaver tip:
Use the julienned broccoli stems in the prepackaged salad section of your supermarket instead of having to wash and cut up broccoli. Or for a quick cabbage coleslaw, buy the bagged coleslaw cabbage mix, add raisins and sunflower seeds and use the dressing from the above recipe.

coleslaw with pineapple

Nutritional analysis per serving:
40 calories
1 g protein
1 g fat
0 g saturated fat
8 g carbohydrate
0 mg cholesterol
89 mg sodium
2 g fibre

Pineapple, sunflower seeds and jicama give a tropical touch to traditional coleslaw. Use sliced water chestnuts if jicama is not available.

3 cups	shredded cabbage	720 mL
1/2 cup	shredded carrots	120 mL
1 cup	jicama peeled and cut into matchstick-size pieces	240 mL
1	green onion, chopped	1
1	12-oz (340-mL) can crushed pineapple, drained (reserve 1/4 cup/60 mL of juice)	1
1/4 cup	fat-free mayonnaise	60 mL
1/4 tsp	ground black pepper	1.2 mL
1/4 tsp	salt	1.2 mL
2 Tbsp	sunflower seeds	30 mL

In medium bowl, combine cabbage, carrots, jicama, green onion and drained pineapple. Set aside.

In small bowl, combine 1/4 cup (60 mL) reserved pineapple juice, mayonnaise, pepper and salt. Whisk together until smooth. Add to cabbage mixture. Add sunflower seeds and mix well. Let sit for at least 1 hour before serving.

Serves 12.

Timesaver tip:
Buy prepared coleslaw mixture in a bag, crushed pineapple and canned sliced water chestnuts—you will have to do no slicing at all!

chickpea salad

Nutrition notes:
Fresh herbs are not only fat-free and very low in sodium, but are also a great way to flavour foods. Cilantro or Chinese parsley is fresh coriander and has a distinct aroma. Some people find cilantro has a strong taste, so you may want to use it in small amounts.

Nutritional analysis per serving:
152 calories
6 g protein
4 g fat
0 g saturated fat
26 g carbohydrate
0 mg cholesterol
468 mg sodium
6 g fibre

Make this salad a few hours ahead of time to let the vegetables marinate. Use parsley instead of cilantro if you prefer.

1	19-oz (540-mL) can chickpeas, drained and rinsed	1
2	tomatoes, chopped	2
1	long English cucumber, diced	1
1	red bell pepper, chopped	1
1/2	purple onion, finely chopped	1/2
2 Tbsp	chopped cilantro	30 mL
1 Tbsp	olive oil	15 mL
3 Tbsp	red wine vinegar	45 mL
1	clove garlic, crushed	1
1/2 tsp	salt	2.5 mL
1/4 tsp	ground black pepper	1.2 mL

Mix chickpeas, tomatoes, cucumber, red pepper, onion and cilantro in bowl. Set aside. Mix oil, vinegar, garlic, salt and pepper in jar. Pour over vegetables and mix. Chill before serving.

Serves 6 as a side dish.

Timesaver tip:
For a quick chickpea salad, mix together canned kidney beans, green beans, chickpeas, diced green bell pepper and onion. Toss with bottled light oil and vinegar dressing.

roasted sweet potato sticks

Nutrition notes:
Yams and sweet potatoes are excellent snacks—they not only provide vitamins and minerals, but are satisfying without excess fat or sugar.

Nutritional analysis per serving:
87 calories
1 g protein
2 g fat
0 g saturated fat
16 g carbohydrate
0 mg cholesterol
6 mg sodium
2 g fibre

Sweet potatoes are yellow when peeled, whereas yams are orange. Either taste great, but sweet potatoes are firmer and keep their shape when served as finger food. Include these sticks in a mixture of grilled vegetables to add an interesting texture.

2	medium sweet potatoes, peeled	2
2 tsp	oil	10 mL
2 tsp	sugar	10 mL

Preheat oven to 375°F (190°C). Cut sweet potatoes into sticks about $1/2$ x 3 in (1.2 x 7.5 cm), similar to french fries. Place in plastic bag. Add oil and shake until oil is evenly distributed over sticks. Add sugar and shake again.

Remove sticks from bag and spread in single layer on non-stick baking sheet. Bake, turning once, for 35 minutes, or until tender and golden.

Serves 4.

Timesaver tip:
Sweet potatoes and yams can be sliced into rounds and baked on cookie sheets without any oil or sugar. These "yam cookies" can be eaten as snacks.

lemon herb potatoes

Nutrition notes:
Leaving potatoes unpeeled doubles their fibre content.

Nutritional analysis per serving:
154 calories
4 g protein
2 g fat
0 g saturated fat
32 g carbohydrate
0 mg cholesterol
351 mg sodium
3 g fibre

Make sure you pour any extra sauce over the potatoes when you serve them, to really enjoy its delicious lemony flavour. This recipe works just as well with nugget potatoes.

2	large yellow potatoes, sliced in eighths	2
$^1/_4$ tsp	salt	1.2 mL
$^1/_4$ tsp	freshly cracked black pepper	1.2 mL
$^3/_4$ tsp	dried oregano	4 mL
1 tsp	olive oil	5 mL
$^1/_2$ cup	chicken broth	120 mL
$^1/_2$	lemon, juiced	$^1/_2$

Preheat oven to 350°F (175°C). Line 9- x 13-in (23- x 33-cm) baking sheet with aluminum foil (leaving enough foil to fold over and make a sealed packet).

Sprinkle potatoes with salt, pepper, oregano and oil. Pour chicken broth over top. Seal foil package. Bake for 45 minutes to 1 hour, or until potatoes are tender. Squeeze lemon juice over potatoes before serving.

Serves 4.

roasted garlic potatoes and yams

Nutrition notes:
Although studies are still inconclusive as to whether garlic will reduce cholesterol levels, mellow roasted garlic is delicious spread on crusty bread.

Nutritional analysis per serving:
166 calories
3 g protein
3 g fat
0 g saturated fat
34 g carbohydrate
0 mg cholesterol
203 mg sodium
3 g fibre

The roasted garlic and rosemary make these potatoes irresistible. Make extras as they will disappear quickly. You can also use diced beets, baby carrots or parsnips.

1³/₄ lbs	nugget potatoes, halved	800 g
1	medium yam, chunked	1
8	mushrooms	8
1 Tbsp	olive oil	15 mL
4	cloves garlic, crushed with skins	4
1¹/₂ tsp	rosemary	7.5 mL
¹/₂ tsp	salt	2.5 mL

Preheat oven to 425°F (220°C). Combine potatoes, yam and mushrooms in a bowl and toss with oil. Spread potatoes cut side down on cast-iron frying pan. Add yam, mushrooms and garlic on top. Sprinkle with rosemary and salt.

Bake uncovered for 45 minutes to 1 hour, or until vegetables are tender. Stir halfway through cooking. Squeeze roasted garlic from skins and discard skins before serving.

Serves 6.

Timesaver tip:
Make an extra pan of these potatoes and save them for making potato salad the next day. Simply toss the vegetables with a vinaigrette dressing.

hash brown potatoes and onions

Nutrition notes:
Make a little oil go a long way. Each tablespoon (15 mL) of oil contains 125 calories and 14 grams of fat. A small amount of oil, though, is needed to add essential fatty acids to our diet and flavour to our food.

Nutritional analysis per serving:
160 calories
3 g protein
3 g fat
0 g saturated fat
32 g carbohydrate
0 mg cholesterol
154 mg sodium
3 g fibre

Onions add a real "fried" taste to these oven-fried potatoes. For special occasions, use whole pearl onions.

4	medium potatoes, peeled and diced into $1/4$-in (.6-cm) cubes	4
1	onion, diced	1
2 tsp	oil	10 mL
$1/4$ tsp	salt	1.2 mL
$1/4$ tsp	ground black pepper	1.2 mL

Preheat oven to 400°F (200°C). Place all ingredients in plastic bag. Shake well until oil, salt and pepper are evenly distributed over vegetables.

Spread vegetables on non-stick baking sheet. Bake for 45 minutes, or until browned, turning potatoes over once with spatula.

Serves 4.

Timesaver tip:
Make ranch-style french fries by cutting unpeeled potato halves into 8 pieces lengthwise. Season and bake as above.

oven-roasted vegetables

Nutrition notes:
Some vegetables may contain more significant amounts of a particular nutrient than another, but there is no one vegetable that is the ultimate choice for maintaining good health. A variety of vegetables should be eaten every day to ensure that you are getting all the nutrients you need.

Nutritional analysis per serving:
92 calories
2 g protein
3 g fat
0 g saturated fat
17 g carbohydrate
0 mg cholesterol
218 mg sodium
4 g fibre

Excellent vegetable accompaniment to almost any dinner entrée! Fennel adds flavour and texture to this interesting mix of vegetables.

2	large carrots, peeled and sliced diagonally $^1/_4$ in (.6 cm) thick	2
2	onions, cut into eighths	2
1	small zucchini, cut in $^1/_2$-in (1.2-cm) slices	1
2	Roma tomatoes, quartered	2
1	bulb fennel, cut into $^1/_2$-in (.6-cm) wedges	1
1	sweet potato, peeled and cut into french fry–style pieces	1
1 Tbsp	olive oil	15 mL
	juice of $^1/_2$ lemon	
$^1/_2$ tsp	salt	2.5 mL
$^1/_4$ tsp	ground black pepper	1.2 mL
2	cloves garlic, minced	2
1 Tbsp	fresh rosemary	15 mL
2 Tbsp	sweet wine (optional)	30 mL

Preheat oven to 400°F (200°C). In medium roasting pan, combine all vegetables. Add oil, lemon juice, salt, pepper, garlic, rosemary and wine, if desired. Mix well with large spoon. Roast uncovered for 45 minutes, stirring occasionally for even roasting.

Serves 6.

Timesaver tip:
If cooking vegetables for every meal seems a real chore, recipes such as these roasted vegetables are the perfect solution. Refrigerate leftovers and eat them the following day, or freeze them in serving-size portions.

roasted lemon maple carrots and rutabaga

Nutrition notes:
Rutabaga is really a cross between turnip and cabbage. Nature has managed one of its tricks when it comes to the potassium in rutabaga— 1 cup (240 mL) of turnip has 211 mg of potassium, cabbage has 172 mg, yet rutabaga has 701 mg!

Nutritional analysis per serving:
72 calories
1 g protein
1 g fat
0 g saturated fat
15 g carbohydrate
0 mg cholesterol
48 mg sodium
4 g fibre

Baking with the cover on speeds up cooking, but also tends to steam the vegetables. Roasting uncovered almost glazes the vegetables. Parsnips and carrots also make a tasty pair.

4	carrots, cut into sticks	4
$1/2$	rutabaga, cut into sticks	$1/2$
1 Tbsp	maple syrup	15 mL
2 Tbsp	lemon juice	30 mL
1 tsp	margarine	5 mL

Preheat oven to 375°F (190°C). Place carrots and rutabaga in small roasting pan. Add maple syrup and lemon juice. Mix vegetables gently to coat with maple syrup and lemon juice. Dot margarine over vegetables.

Bake uncovered for 30 minutes, or until vegetables are done. Mix vegetables once while cooking.

Serves 4.

Timesaver tip:
Use packaged prewashed baby carrots, and omit the rutabaga.

collard greens with honey lemon dressing

Nutrition notes:
If it is not possible to get your favourite flavour in the lighter version of a vinaigrette salad dressing, make a touch of regular dressing go a long way. Use just a very small amount, or dilute the regular dressing with an equal amount of rice or balsamic vinegar.

Nutritional analysis per serving:
114 calories
3 g protein
5 g fat
1 g saturated fat
11 g carbohydrate
0 mg cholesterol
113 mg sodium
3 g fibre

This honey lemon dressing enhances the flavour of almost any cooked vegetable or mixture of salad greens. Try the dressing with mesclun greens and sliced, vine-ripened tomatoes for an especially tasty salad. You can vary the nut, too—toasted slivered almonds or sunflower seeds are good alternatives.

1 lb	collard greens	450 g
1 Tbsp	olive oil	15 mL
	juice of 1 lemon	
1 1/2 Tbsp	honey	22.5 mL
1/8 tsp	salt	.5 mL
2 tsp	Dijon mustard	10 mL
2 Tbsp	toasted hazelnuts, coarsely chopped	30 mL

Trim off and discard ends of collard greens and boil greens in small amount of water until tender. Drain. Cut into serving-sized pieces and place in serving dish.

Combine oil, lemon juice, honey, salt and mustard in small jar. Shake well and pour over collard greens. Sprinkle with hazelnuts and toss.

Serves 4.

Timesaver tip:
To perk up the flavour of boiled vegetables, add a little of your favourite commercial light vinaigrette dressing and toss. If you have more time one day of the week, make a double portion of a low-fat dressing and keep it handy in the refrigerator.

carrots and green beans with lemon dill

Nutrition notes:
Although many vitamins are better preserved when food is uncooked, the beta-carotene in carrots is more readily available to our bodies when carrots are cooked.

Nutritional analysis per serving:
55 calories
2 g protein
1 g fat
0 g saturated fat
11 g carbohydrate
0 mg cholesterol
94 mg sodium
4 g fibre

Eye appeal is almost as important as the flavour of a dish. Although it might take just a little more time, cutting carrots into thin slices that match the green beans in size enhances the eye appeal of this vegetable duo.

1/2 lb	carrots, peeled	225 g
1/2 lb	green beans	225 g
1 tsp	olive oil	5 mL
1 Tbsp	lemon juice	15 mL
1 Tbsp	chopped fresh dill	15 mL
1/8 tsp	salt	.5 mL
1/8 tsp	ground black pepper	.5 mL

Cut carrots into thin sticks the same length as the green beans. Place carrots and green beans in small amount of water in covered pot and boil for 5 minutes, or until just tender. Drain. Add olive oil, lemon juice, dill, salt and pepper and mix gently.

Serves 4.

Timesaver tip:
Omit the carrots and make the dish with frozen green beans. Be careful not to overcook them—keep in mind that they have already been slightly precooked.

beets with a bite

Nutrition notes:
Bananas watch out! Beet roots contain 800 mg potassium per cup (240 mL), while cooked beet greens have 1300 mg potassium. A banana, the traditional high-potassium food, contains 450 mg of potassium.

Nutritional analysis per serving:
117 calories
3 g protein
5 g fat
1 g saturated fat
17 g carbohydrate
2 mg cholesterol
139 mg sodium
5 g fibre

A nice change from the traditional Harvard beets. The horseradish gives the beets a little zip. Serve them slightly warmed for the best taste.

4	large beets, peeled	4
1 Tbsp	olive oil	15 mL
2 Tbsp	hot water	30 mL
1$\frac{1}{2}$ Tbsp	creamy horseradish	22.5 mL
1 tsp	red wine vinegar	5 mL

Slice beets into serving-sized chunks. Place beets in large pot and cover with water. Bring to a boil. Continue to simmer until beets are tender. Drain beets and put in serving dish.

Mix oil, water, horseradish and vinegar together. Pour over beets and stir.

Serves 4.

Timesaver tip:
For a quick version, use canned sliced beets. Warm and toss with remaining ingredients.

asparagus vinaigrette

Nutrition notes:
Steaming preserves the texture, flavour and most of the vitamins and minerals in food.

Nutritional analysis per serving:
59 calories
3 g protein
4 g fat
1 g saturated fat
3 g carbohydrate
0 mg cholesterol
95 mg sodium
1 g fibre

This is a delicious side dish for a spring barbecue. It's easy to prepare and can be made ahead of time.

1 lb	asparagus	450 g
1½ Tbsp	red wine vinegar	22.5 mL
1 Tbsp	balsamic vinegar	15 mL
1 Tbsp	olive oil	15 mL
1 tsp	Dijon mustard	5 mL
⅛ tsp	salt	.5 mL
⅛ tsp	ground black pepper	.5 mL

Snap tough ends off asparagus. Steam asparagus until tender-crisp. Combine wine vinegar, balsamic vinegar, oil, mustard, salt and pepper in a small jar and shake. Pour over asparagus.

Marinate for at least 2 hours in the refrigerator before serving, stirring after 1 hour.

Serves 4.

pan-seared asparagus

Nutrition notes:
Asparagus is rich in folic acid; a 1-cup (240-mL) serving contains over one-half of your daily recommended intake.

Searing asparagus gives it a delicious, almost nutty flavour. Make sure you choose spears that are not too thick—about the thickness of a pencil is best when prepared this way.

1 lb	asparagus	450 g
1 tsp	olive oil	5 mL
$^{1}/_{4}$ tsp	coarse salt	1.2 mL
	ground black pepper to taste	

Nutritional analysis per serving:
36 calories
3 g protein
2 g fat
0 g saturated fat
2 g carbohydrate
0 mg cholesterol
160 mg sodium
1 g fibre

Snap the lower part of the asparagus off. Place asparagus spears in sink full of cold water. Place a well-seasoned cast-iron frying pan on high heat. Move asparagus directly from sink into heated frying pan. Turn asparagus with tongs and cook until tender and slightly browned, about 5–10 minutes.

Remove with tongs to a plate. Drizzle with oil and sprinkle with salt and pepper.

Serves 4.

brunches and light meals

salmon salad

Nutrition notes:
The creator of this recipe says that a great salad is made with anything red, green, yellow and/or orange. He is absolutely correct—those bright colours tell us the salad is rich in antioxidants, such as beta-carotene and lycopenes.

Nutritional analysis per serving:
157 calories
11 g protein
9 g fat
2 g saturated fat
8 g carbohydrate
13 mg cholesterol
258 mg sodium
2 g fibre

Serve this great main-course salad for lunch, along with fresh crusty rolls and a lemon sorbet for dessert. Any type of canned salmon can be used, but red sockeye salmon gives the salad extra colour.

1	7^1/2-oz (213-g) can sockeye salmon	1
1 Tbsp	Dijon mustard	15 mL
1 Tbsp	olive oil	15 mL
2 Tbsp	apple juice	30 mL
2 Tbsp	apple cider vinegar	30 mL
1	clove garlic, crushed	1
	salt and ground black pepper to taste	
1	head butter lettuce	1
1	head red leaf lettuce	1
1	tomato, diced	1
1	carrot, shredded	1

Drain salmon, reserving liquid. Set salmon aside. Combine liquid from canned salmon with mustard, oil, juice, vinegar, garlic, salt and pepper. Shake or whisk together well.

To prepare salad, tear butter lettuce and red leaf lettuce into bite-sized pieces. Place in large salad bowl. Add diced tomato and shredded carrot. Crumble salmon on top of vegetables. Pour dressing over salad and toss.

Serves 4.

Timesaver tip:
Use prepackaged salad greens instead of the lettuces. Mesclun mix is especially delicious.

seared scallop salad

Nutrition notes:
Despite popular belief, not all seafood is high in dietary cholesterol. Scallops, clams, mussels and oysters are low in both fat and cholesterol.

Nutritional analysis per serving:
162 calories
17 g protein
8 g fat
1 g saturated fat
6 g carbohydrate
28 mg cholesterol
453 mg sodium
2 g fibre

Be sure you use the large meaty sea scallops rather than the small bay scallops. They are expensive, but are truly delicious for a special treat. Sprinkle salads with freshly cracked pepper and finely grated Parmesan cheese before serving.

5 cups	mixed greens, such as red leaf lettuce, arugula and spinach	1.2 L
4	large fresh sea scallops (about 6 oz/170 g)	4
1 tsp	Dijon mustard	5 mL
1 Tbsp	olive oil	15 mL
2 Tbsp	red wine vinegar	30 mL
1 Tbsp	fresh lemon juice	15 mL
	salt and ground black pepper to taste	

Tear lettuce into small pieces and put into large salad bowl. To sear scallops, spray a ridged non-stick grill pan or frying pan with olive oil. Place over high heat. Add scallops to hot skillet. Scallops should sizzle when placed in pan. Reduce heat slightly. Resist temptation to turn scallops too soon—wait until they are brown on one side and firm to the touch, about 4 minutes. Turn over and turn off heat. Let sit 1 minute. Do not overcook.

Meanwhile, put remaining ingredients into glass jar and shake well. Toss greens with dressing. Place salad on large plates and top each serving with 2 scallops.

Serves 2.

Timesaver tip:
For a less expensive, quick seafood salad, substitute imitation or canned crab for the scallops.

salad niçoise with pesto dressing

Nutrition notes:
Canned water-packed tuna has only 100 calories in 3 oz (85 g), yet contains just as much protein as processed meats. That makes tuna a good choice for a lighter lunch.

Nutritional analysis per serving:
336 calories
31 g protein
6 g fat
1 g saturated fat
40 g carbohydrate
58 mg cholesterol
748 mg sodium
8 g fibre

This salad is great for a summer luncheon. Serve it with fresh buns and fruit crisp for dessert.

1	yellow bell pepper	1
2	6$^{1}/_{2}$-oz (184-g) cans solid water-packed tuna, drained	2
3 cups	mixed greens	720 mL
3 cups	spinach, torn	720 mL
12	cherry tomatoes, halved	12
12	nugget potatoes, boiled and halved	12
$^{3}/_{4}$ lb	green beans, blanched and cut in bite-sized pieces	340 g
1 cup	basil leaves, loosely packed	240 mL
2 Tbsp	red wine vinegar	30 mL
1 Tbsp	balsamic vinegar	15 mL
2 Tbsp	water	30 mL
$^{1}/_{4}$ tsp	salt	1.2 mL
$^{1}/_{8}$ tsp	ground black pepper	.5 mL
1 Tbsp	olive oil	15 mL
8	kalamata olives	8

Heat oven to 375°F (190°C). Bake whole yellow pepper on baking sheet 45 minutes, or until skin is blistered and slightly darkened. Peel off skin when cool enough to handle. Cut pepper into chunks.

Break tuna into small chunks and place in large bowl. Add mixed greens, spinach, tomatoes, roasted pepper, potatoes and beans. Set aside.

Place basil, wine and balsamic vinegars, water, salt and pepper into food processor or blender and purée until smooth. Add oil and purée until mixed. Toss dressing with salad. Divide salad among 4 plates and top each serving with 2 olives.

Serves 4.

tuna melts

Nutrition notes:
Water-packed tuna is high in protein, low in calories and contains only 1 gram of fat per 3 oz (85 g). Oil-packed tuna, on the other hand, has 7 grams of fat, even after the oil is drained.

Nutritional analysis per serving:
192 calories
19 g protein
4 g fat
2 g saturated fat
19 g carbohydrate
18 mg cholesterol
560 mg sodium
2 g fibre

A delicious change from the usual tuna sandwich. The firm texture of rye bread provides a solid base for the substantial filling in this open-faced sandwich, but any other bread can be used.

1	6$^{1}/_{2}$-oz (184-g) can water-packed tuna	1
1 Tbsp	lemon juice	15 mL
1 Tbsp	chopped fresh dill	15 mL
2 Tbsp	fat-free mayonnaise	30 mL
$^{1}/_{4}$ cup	1% cottage cheese	60 mL
4	slices rye bread	4
1	large tomato, sliced	1
2 oz	light mozzarella cheese, shredded	57 g
2 Tbsp	grated light Parmesan cheese	30 mL

Preheat oven to 400°F (200°C). Combine tuna, lemon juice, dill, mayonnaise and cottage cheese. Mix well. Spread evenly on bread slices. Top with tomato slices. Sprinkle with cheeses. Place slices on baking sheet and bake for 10 minutes, or until cheese is melted and bread is slightly toasted.

Serves 4.

tuna broccoli casserole

Nutrition notes:
Pasta by itself is calorie-dense, with 200 calories in just 1 cup (240 mL) of cooked pasta. Adding lots of vegetables to pasta dishes helps stretch the pasta.

Nutritional analysis per serving:
384 calories
25 g protein
8 g fat
2 g saturated fat
52 g carbohydrate
33 mg cholesterol
780 mg sodium
5 g fibre

This is true comfort food with a boost of broccoli for extra nutrition.

2 cups	broccoli florets, slightly cooked	475 mL
1	6$\frac{1}{2}$-oz (184-g) can water-packed tuna, drained	1
4 cups	cooked rotini	950 mL
$\frac{1}{2}$ cup	chopped celery	120 mL
$\frac{1}{2}$	medium onion, chopped	$\frac{1}{2}$
1	10-oz (284-g) can light cream of mushroom soup	1
$\frac{3}{4}$ cup	skim milk	180 mL
$\frac{1}{4}$ cup	grated low-fat Cheddar cheese	60 mL

Preheat oven to 350°F (175°C). Layer broccoli in bottom of 2-qt (2-L) covered casserole dish. Set aside. In large bowl, combine tuna, rotini, celery and onion. Mix well. In small bowl, whisk together mushroom soup and skim milk. Add to rotini mixture and stir.

Put rotini mixture on top of broccoli in casserole dish. Do not stir. Sprinkle with grated cheese. Cover and bake for 45 minutes.

Serves 4.

Timesaver tip:
Simply replace the broccoli with 2 cups (475 mL) of frozen vegetable mixture.

crustless salmon quiche

Nutrition notes:
Industry is responding to the needs of the public for eggs with lower cholesterol. Where eggs are the primary ingredient, such as in omelettes, quiches, frittatas and custards, cholesterol-reduced eggs provide an excellent substitute for regular eggs.

Nutritional analysis per serving:
193 calories
20 g protein
6 g fat
3 g saturated fat
13 g carbohydrate
13 g cholesterol
34 mg sodium
1 g fibre

Quiche without a crust is like a frittata baked in a pie plate. Vary this recipe by using different kinds of low-fat cheeses or adding other vegetables, such as chopped broccoli. Cartons of cholesterol-reduced eggs are usually found next to the fresh whole eggs in the supermarket.

1	7^1/2-oz (213-g) can pink salmon	1
1^1/2 cups	skim milk	360 mL
1 cup	cholesterol-reduced eggs	240 mL
^{1}/2 cup	flour	120 mL
1 cup	grated light Cheddar cheese	240 mL
2 cups	coarsely chopped spinach, loosely packed	475 mL
^{1}/4 cup	chopped green onions	60 mL

Preheat oven to 400°F (200°C). Drain salmon, reserving liquid. Crumble salmon chunks into small pieces, crushing bones. Set aside.

In mixing bowl, combine liquid from salmon, skim milk, eggs and flour. Beat well with electric mixer until smooth. Pour into greased 9^1/2-in (24-cm) deep pie plate. Sprinkle with cheese, salmon, spinach and green onions. With a fork, press solid ingredients down into liquid mixture. Bake for 45 minutes, or until knife inserted in middle comes out clean. Let sit for 10 minutes before cutting.

Serves 6.

Timesaver tip:
Having no crust or eggs to beat up simplifies this quiche tremendously, but for even less preparation time, buy prewashed spinach leaves and pregrated cheese.

seafood lasagna

Nutrition notes:
Using skim milk to make a white sauce, rather than a tomato-based sauce, adds extra calcium to this dish. The white sauce mixed with a little Parmesan cheese also gives the illusion of more cheese, without the saturated fat content of regular cheese.

Nutritional analysis per serving:
418 calories
38 g protein
6 g fat
3 g saturated fat
52 g carbohydrate
67 mg cholesterol
1296 mg sodium
4 g fibre

. For special occasions, use real crab instead of imitation crab.

$2^3/4$ cups	skim milk	660 mL
$1/4$ cup	flour	60 mL
$1/2$ tsp	salt	2.5 mL
$1/2$ tsp	garlic powder	2.5 mL
$1^1/2$ cups	1% cottage cheese	360 mL
1	egg	1
$1/2$ cup	light Parmesan cheese	120 mL
$1/4$ tsp	ground black pepper	1.2 mL
1	10-oz (284-g) pkg chopped frozen spinach, thawed and drained	1
$3/4$ lb	imitation crab, coarsely chopped	340 g
1	$6^1/2$-oz (184-g) can water-packed tuna, drained and broken up	1
$1/4$ cup	chopped green onions	60 mL
9	lasagna noodles, cooked	9
2 Tbsp	light Parmesan cheese	30 mL

Preheat oven to 350°F (175°C). In small pan, whisk together milk, flour, salt and garlic powder to make a white sauce. Bring to boil over medium heat, stirring constantly until thickened. Remove from heat and set aside.

In medium bowl, combine cottage cheese, egg, $1/2$ cup (120 mL) Parmesan cheese and pepper. Mix well. Set aside.

Squeeze water from spinach. In medium bowl, combine spinach, imitation crab, tuna and green onions. Set aside.

To assemble lasagna, spread about ¹/₄ cup (60 mL) white sauce on bottom of 9- x 13-in (23- x 33-cm) lasagna pan. Line pan with 3 cooked lasagna noodles. Spread ¹/₂ cottage cheese mixture evenly on top of noodles. Spread ¹/₂ spinach mixture over top. Pour ¹/₃ remaining white sauce over top.

Repeat with another layer of noodles, cottage cheese mixture, spinach mixture and sauce. Cover with last 3 lasagna noodles and remaining sauce. Sprinkle with 2 Tbsp (30 mL) Parmesan cheese.

Bake for 40–45 minutes uncovered, or until mixture is bubbly. Let sit for 10 minutes before cutting.

Serves 6.

Timesaver tip:
If you like the flavour of seafood and pasta in a white sauce, but putting together a lasagna is not in your schedule, opt for a seafood casserole. Use pasta such as penne and a can of low-fat cream of mushroom soup diluted with milk. Add tuna and imitation crabmeat along with chopped celery and green onions. Bake in a covered casserole dish for 30 minutes, or until casserole is heated through.

black bean quesadillas

Nutrition notes:
The Mexican word for sauce is salsa. Salsa can be fresh, cooked or canned and can range in spiciness from very mild to mouth-burning. Fresh tomato salsa, unlike creamy sauces, is not only low in fat, but also rich in lycopenes and vitamin C.

Nutritional analysis per serving:
241 calories
11 g protein
6 g fat
2 g saturated fat
36 g carbohydrate
8 mg cholesterol
633 mg sodium
6 g fibre

For a heartier meal, add leftover chicken to these quesadillas. Serve them with salsa and low-fat plain yogurt. To serve quesadillas as an appetizer, cut them into smaller wedges.

1 tsp	oil	5 mL
$^1/_2$	small onion, chopped	$^1/_2$
3	cloves garlic, minced	3
$^1/_2$ tsp	chili powder	2.5 mL
1 tsp	ground cumin	5 mL
1	19-oz (540-mL) can black beans, drained and rinsed	1
1	19-oz (540-mL) can diced tomatoes, drained	1
$^1/_2$ cup	salsa	120 mL
$^1/_3$ cup	chopped cilantro	80 mL
1 Tbsp	lime juice	15 mL
8	8-in (20-cm) flour tortillas	8
4 oz	part-skim Cheddar cheese, grated	113 g

Heat oil over medium heat in medium non-stick frying pan. Add onion, garlic, chili powder and cumin. Sauté until onions are soft. Add black beans, tomatoes, salsa and cilantro. Sauté until heated through. Remove from heat. Add lime juice.

Spread $^1/_4$ of mixture onto each of 4 tortillas. Sprinkle each with grated cheese. Top each with another tortilla. In non-stick pan, over low heat, cook each quesadilla until browned. Flip over and heat other side. Cut each into quarters and serve.

Serves 8.

Timesaver tip:
For a quick bean quesadilla, buy vegetarian refried beans. Spread beans, salsa and low-fat grated cheese onto tortilla. Top with another tortilla. Heat in oven until cheese is melted.

oriental chicken pilaf

Nutrition notes:
Just 1 Tbsp (15 mL) of sodium-reduced soy sauce contains over 500 mg of sodium. To keep sodium intake down, use it only very sparingly.

Nutritional analysis per serving:
442 calories
17 g protein
2 g fat
0 g saturated fat
86 g carbohydrate
25 mg cholesterol
443 mg sodium
4 g fibre

Dried shiitake mushrooms add an interesting flavour to this dish. They can be purchased in most supermarkets that carry Asian ingredients.

3 cups	short-grain rice	720 mL
3 cups	water	720 mL
4	dried shiitake mushrooms	4
1	whole boneless skinless chicken breast, diced	1
2	carrots, diced into 1/4-in (.6-cm) pieces	2
1	8-oz (227-mL) can sliced water chestnuts, drained and coarsely chopped	1
1½ cups	water	360 mL
¼ cup	sodium-reduced soy sauce	60 mL
2 Tbsp	sweet wine	30 mL
1 Tbsp	brown sugar	15 mL

Wash rice and drain well. In a covered, medium pot, bring rice and 3 cups (720 mL) water to a boil. Reduce heat to low and cook, covered, until rice is done, about 15 minutes.

Meanwhile, soak shiitake mushrooms in warm water until softened, about 15 minutes. Drain. Remove and discard stems. Cut mushroom caps into thin strips. Put into medium pot along with diced chicken, carrots and water chestnuts. Add 1½ cups (360 mL) water, soy sauce, wine and sugar. Bring to a boil, and cook over medium heat until vegetables and chicken are cooked.

Put cooked hot rice into large serving bowl. Add chicken mixture and liquid and mix gently until rice is coated.

Serves 6.

sushi salad

Nutrition notes:
Although sushi can be low in fat, it is not necessarily low in calories. Each cup of cooked rice has 230 calories, so large amounts of sushi can add up quite quickly. Remember to eat a balanced diet at each meal, with servings from at least 3 groups in Canada's Food Guide.

Nutritional analysis per serving:
427 calories
15 g protein
2 g fat
0 g saturated fat
85 g carbohydrate
0 mg cholesterol
577 mg sodium
4 g fibre

This salad boasts the flavour of sushi without the hassle of making rolls. Vary the toppings by using bean sprouts, blanched snow peas or shredded white radish. Nori is the black seaweed used in making sushi rolls and can be purchased in most Asian stores. Keep leftover nori in an airtight container to maintain crispness.

2 cups	short-grain Japanese-type rice	475 mL
2 cups	water	475 mL
3 Tbsp	rice vinegar	45 mL
2 Tbsp	sugar	30 mL
1/2 tsp	salt	2.5 mL
1 Tbsp	toasted sesame seeds	15 mL
4	leaves leaf lettuce	4
1	carrot, shredded	1
$^1/_4$	long English cucumber, julienned	$^1/_4$
$^1/_2$ lb	cooked shrimp or crabmeat	225 g
1	sheet toasted nori, cut into $^1/_8$- x 2-in (.5- x 5-cm) strips	1

Wash rice and drain well. In a covered, medium pot, bring rice and water to a boil. Reduce heat to low and cook until done, about 15 minutes (or cook in rice cooker). Put hot rice into large bowl.

In small bowl, combine vinegar, sugar and salt. Mix well. Pour mixture over hot rice. Mix gently, with a folding motion, until vinegar mixture is evenly distributed throughout rice. Fanning rice until cool while mixing gently will help keep sushi rice shiny and less sticky. Stir in sesame seeds.

To assemble, place one lettuce leaf on each of 4 individual salad plates. Divide sushi rice evenly onto lettuce leaves. Sprinkle each rice serving with carrot, cucumber and shrimp. Top with nori strips.

Serves 4.

fried rice and vegetables

Nutrition notes:
Frying food doesn't necessarily mean high fat when cooking at home. A little oil can go a long way in adding a fried flavour to a dish. Just make sure you use a non-stick frying pan.

Nutritional analysis per serving:
366 calories
11 g protein
4 g fat
1 g saturated fat
71 g carbohydrate
8 mg cholesterol
396 mg sodium
3 g fibre

"Everything but the kitchen sink" is a good description for this dish. You can use any vegetable, any leftover cooked meat or poultry or even cubed firm tofu instead of meat. It's a great way to use up leftovers and bits of vegetables in the fridge.

1 Tbsp	oil	15 mL
1/2	onion, chopped	1/2
1/2 cup	coarsely chopped celery	120 mL
1/2 cup	cooked ham, diced	120 mL
1 cup	diced zucchini	240 mL
5 cups	cooked rice	1.2 L
1/2 cup	frozen peas	120 mL
1	12-oz (340-mL) can corn kernels, drained	1
1/4 tsp	salt	1.2 mL

Heat oil in large non-stick frying pan over medium heat. Add onion and celery and sauté until onions are golden. Add ham and zucchini. Sauté and stir until zucchini is softened and ham is hot.

Reduce heat to low. Add cooked rice, frozen peas, corn and salt. Mix well. Cook covered, stirring occasionally to prevent sticking, until rice is hot.

Serves 5.

banana pancakes

Nutrition notes:
To increase the fibre, use a mixture of whole-wheat and white flour.

Nutritional analysis per 2 pancakes:
206 calories
6 g protein
5 g fat
1 g saturated fat
35 g carbohydrate
61 mg cholesterol
477 mg sodium
3 g fibre

This is a favourite weekend breakfast dish. Top with yogurt, maple syrup or fruit purée. If you prefer, add sliced strawberries, raspberries or blueberries instead of bananas.

2 cups	flour, sifted	475 mL
2 tsp	sugar	10 mL
$^1/_2$ tsp	salt	2.5 mL
$1^1/_2$ tsp	baking powder	7.5 mL
1 tsp	baking soda	5 mL
2	eggs	2
2 cups	low-fat buttermilk	475 mL
2 Tbsp	margarine, melted	30 mL
2	bananas, sliced into rounds	2

In medium bowl, sift flour, sugar, salt, baking powder and baking soda. Set aside. Beat eggs until light in colour. Add buttermilk to eggs and beat. Combine liquid and sifted ingredients together and mix until moistened. Stir in melted margarine.

Heat non-stick skillet over high heat. Add a few drops of water to pan—if water sizzles, pan is ready. Using $^1/_4$-cup (60-mL) ladle, drop batter onto hot pan. Top each pancake with 3 slices banana. When bubbles appear, pancakes are ready to flip over. Continue to cook until second side has browned. Top with favourite pancake topping.

Makes 16 pancakes.

Timesaver tip:
Save leftovers in the fridge, and pop them in the toaster oven for a quick snack or breakfast the next day.

pastas and grains

penne with vegetables and sun-dried tomatoes

Nutrition notes:
Sun-dried tomatoes that are marinated in olive oil are very high in fat, so make sure you rinse them off before adding them to a recipe. Sun-dried tomatoes that are not marinated are much lower in fat, yet very flavourful. Soak them in boiling water to soften them before using.

Nutritional analysis per side dish serving:
145 calories
6 g protein
4 g fat
1 g saturated fat
24 g carbohydrate
1 mg cholesterol
103 mg sodium
4 g fibre

Serve this dish warm, as an accompaniment to a main course, such as grilled chicken, or as a cold pasta salad for lunch.

1/2 cup	sun-dried tomatoes (not oil-packed)	120 mL
2 Tbsp	olive oil	30 mL
6	cloves garlic, chopped	6
3	tomatoes, diced	3
1/4 tsp	red pepper flakes	1.2 mL
1/4 tsp	salt	1.2 mL
1/8 tsp	ground black pepper	.5 mL
3 cups	broccoli florets, cooked	720 mL
3 cups	cauliflower florets, cooked	720 mL
3/4 lb	dried penne, cooked	340 g
1/4 cup	grated Parmesan cheese	60 mL
1/3 cup	chopped fresh basil	80 mL

Pour boiling water over sun-dried tomatoes and let sit for 15 minutes. Drain and cut into lengthwise strips. Set aside.

Heat oil in large pot. Add garlic and sauté for about 2 minutes. Add sun-dried tomatoes, fresh tomatoes, red pepper flakes, salt, pepper, broccoli and cauliflower. Cook until heated through. Add cooked penne. Add Parmesan cheese and basil and toss until well blended.

Serves 12 as a side dish.

Timesaver tip:
Keep frozen vegetables on hand to use in recipes calling for cooked vegetables. Just remember frozen vegetables are precooked and require very little cooking time.

fettuccine with spinach and tomato sauce

Nutrition notes:
Fettuccine is traditionally served with a creamy Alfredo sauce that is laden with calories and saturated fat. Tomato or other vegetable-based sauces are much lower in fat, yet packed with more flavonoids and other antioxidants.

Nutritional analysis per serving:
365 calories
14 g protein
4 g fat
1 g saturated fat
66 g carbohydrate
1 mg cholesterol
472 mg sodium
5 g fibre

Serve this vegetable-laden pasta with a large tossed salad of mixed greens and you will have almost all your vegetable servings for the day!

1 Tbsp	olive oil	15 mL
1/2	onion, finely chopped	1/2
1/2 cup	finely chopped celery	120 mL
1/4 cup	finely chopped carrot	60 mL
1 lb	fresh spinach, trimmed and coarsely chopped	450 g
1/4 tsp	salt	1.2 mL
1/4 tsp	ground black pepper	1.2 mL
1	28-oz (796-mL) can plum tomatoes, crushed	1
1 lb	dried fettuccine, cooked	450 g
2 Tbsp	freshly grated Parmesan cheese	30 mL

Heat oil in sauté pan over medium heat. Add onions and cook until golden. Add celery and carrots and cook for 2 minutes. Add spinach a handful at a time, stirring as it cooks. Continue until all spinach has been added. Add salt and pepper. Turn heat up to high and continue to cook until all liquid has evaporated, about 10 minutes. Stir to ensure spinach is not sticking.

Add tomatoes and simmer for 10 minutes. Toss with cooked pasta. Top each bowl with a spoonful of Parmesan cheese before serving.

Serves 6.

Timesaver tip:
Buy vegetarian pasta sauce, add fresh chopped spinach, and heat until spinach is cooked. Toss with your favourite pasta and top with Parmesan cheese.

fusilli with eggplant tomato sauce

Nutrition notes:
Eggplants boast of their flavonoid content with their bold purple skin. Next time you are barbecuing, add some eggplants to the grill. Slice large eggplants into thin rounds, brush with olive oil and grill until lightly browned on both sides. Slice Japanese eggplants into halves lengthwise and brush with teriyaki or hoisin sauce. Grill until cooked through.

Nutritional analysis per serving:
376 calories
12 g protein
5 g fat
1 g saturated fat
69 g carbohydrate
0 mg cholesterol
474 mg sodium
5 g fibre

This light, refreshing sauce is delicious over fusilli or rotini. The eggplant gives it a "meaty" texture. This recipe calls for a peeled pepper—the easiest way to peel a pepper is with a vegetable peeler.

1	medium eggplant	1
1 Tbsp	olive oil	15 mL
2	cloves garlic, peeled and thinly sliced	2
	pinch red pepper flakes	
2 Tbsp	fresh parsley	30 mL
$^1/_2$	medium onion, thinly sliced	$^1/_2$
1	yellow or red bell pepper, peeled, cut into strips	1
1	28-oz (796-mL) can plum tomatoes	1
$^1/_3$ cup	dry white wine	80 mL
6	fresh basil leaves, torn	6
$^1/_4$ cup	pitted, diced kalamata olives	60 mL
2 Tbsp	capers, rinsed	30 mL
1 lb	dried fusilli, cooked	450 g

Wash eggplant and cut away top and bottom. Split in half lengthwise. Remove any dark seeds or clusters of seeds. Cut into 3- x 1-in (7.5- x 2.5-cm) pieces. Place eggplant in colander and sprinkle with salt. Place over bowl to catch any liquid and let sit for $^1/_2$ hour to remove any bitter taste.

Heat oil in medium sauté pan over medium heat. Sauté garlic and red pepper flakes for 2 minutes, being careful not to burn garlic. Remove garlic and discard.

Stir in parsley. Add onion and sauté until onion is soft. Add bell pepper and cook until all ingredients are tender. Add eggplant, tomatoes, wine, basil, olives and capers. Cover and simmer for about 45 minutes. If sauce becomes dry, add water. Toss pasta and sauce together and serve.

Serves 6.

Timesaver tip:
Sauté onion, garlic and red pepper flakes until onions are soft. Add all other sauce ingredients and cook covered for 45 minutes. The flavour may not be quite as mellow as with the original recipe, but this simplified version may leave you more hands-free time.

roasted tomato sauce with linguine

Nutrition notes:
Lycopenes are an antioxidant that are plentiful in tomatoes, both raw and cooked.

Nutritional analysis per serving:
346 calories
11 g protein
5 g fat
1 g saturated fat
64 g carbohydrate
0 mg cholesterol
518 mg sodium
4 g fibre

Make this sauce when you have lots of vine-ripened tomatoes.

4	cloves garlic, minced	4
1	medium onion, chopped	1
1/2 cup	kalamata olives, pitted and sliced	120 mL
1/4 cup	capers, rinsed	60 mL
1 tsp	fresh thyme leaves	5 mL
	dash hot pepper sauce	
1 Tbsp	olive oil	15 mL
4	beefsteak tomatoes (about 2 lbs/900 g)	4
	salt and ground black pepper to taste	
1 lb	dried linguine, cooked	450 g

Preheat oven to 450°F (230°C). In a medium baking pan, large enough to hold tomato halves without overlapping, combine garlic, onion, olives, capers, thyme and hot pepper sauce. Drizzle with oil and spread evenly in pan. Remove stem ends from tomatoes and halve crosswise. Arrange cut side down on top of ingredients in pan. Roast 20–25 minutes or until tomato skins blister. Cool in pan about 15 minutes, then remove skins and discard. Add salt and pepper to taste. Blend sauce or mash with potato masher to desired consistency. Toss pasta with sauce before serving.

Serves 6.

Timesaver tip:
Sauté onions and add ready-made chunky pasta sauce. Add chopped olives, capers and a dash of hot pepper sauce. Serve with linguine.

classic tomato sauce with penne

Nutrition notes:
Although pasta is virtually fat-free, the calories add up quickly. A dinner-sized portion should be the size of about 2 fists. Round out a pasta meal with foods from other food groups, such as grilled vegetables or salad, and a glass of low-fat milk.

Nutritional analysis per serving:
404 calories
13 g protein
6 g fat
1 g saturated fat
74 g carbohydrate
0 mg cholesterol
380 mg sodium
6 g fibre

This robust pasta sauce is delicious with any pasta. You can make the sauce ahead of time, as it becomes more flavourful the longer it sits. It is important to sauté the tomato paste with the herbs for a sweet sauce.

2 Tbsp	olive oil	30 mL
$1/2$	onion, finely chopped	$1/2$
3	cloves garlic, crushed	3
$1/3$ cup	chopped fresh parsley	80 mL
1 tsp	dried oregano	5 mL
1 tsp	dried basil	5 mL
2	bay leaves	2
1	$5^1/2$-oz (156-mL) can tomato paste	1
1	14-oz (398-mL) can crushed tomatoes	1
1	14-oz (398-mL) can stewed tomatoes	1
2 tsp	sugar	10 mL
1 lb	dried penne, cooked	450 g

Heat oil in saucepan over medium heat. Add onion and garlic and sauté until onion is translucent, about 5 minutes. Add parsley, oregano, basil and bay leaves and cook for 2 minutes. Add tomato paste. Sauté for 3 minutes. Add crushed and stewed tomatoes and sugar, mixing well.

Cover and simmer over low heat for 30 minutes, stirring frequently to prevent sticking. Remove bay leaves. Toss pasta with sauce before serving.

Serves 6.

artichoke and chickpea rotini salad

Nutrition notes:
The asparagus and garbanzo beans in this salad provide a large portion of the folic acid you need in one day.

Nutritional analysis per serving:
384 calories
14 g protein
7 g fat
2 g saturated fat
65 g carbohydrate
6 mg cholesterol
563 mg sodium
5 g fibre

Chickpeas (also called garbanzo beans), add texture, protein and folic acid to this nutrition-packed salad.

1 lb	dried tricolour rotini pasta, cooked	450 g
1	14-oz (398-mL) can artichoke hearts, drained and quartered	1
1	19-oz (540-mL) can chickpeas, drained and rinsed	1
1	red bell pepper, cut into thin 1-in (2.5-cm) strips	1
2 oz	feta cheese	57 g
2 Tbsp	chopped fresh parsley	30 mL
1 tsp	olive oil	5 mL
1/2 lb	asparagus, cut diagonally into 1-in (2.5-cm) lengths (tough ends broken off)	225 g
2	cloves garlic, minced	2
2 Tbsp	olive oil	30 mL
1/4 cup	balsamic vinegar	60 mL
1/2 tsp	salt	2.5 mL
1/4 tsp	ground black pepper	1.2 mL
2 tsp	dried oregano	10 mL

Place cooked pasta in large mixing bowl. Add artichoke hearts, chickpeas, red pepper, feta cheese and parsley. Set aside.

Heat 1 tsp (5 mL) oil in non-stick frying pan over medium-high heat. Add asparagus and cook until just seared and bright green. Add to pasta mixture.

Timesaver tip:
Omit asparagus, and use any raw vegetable you have, such as carrots, Roma tomatoes or zucchini. A commercial calorie-reduced Italian or balsamic vinegar dressing can be substituted for this dressing.

Combine garlic, 2 Tbsp (30 mL) oil, vinegar, salt, pepper and oregano in small jar and shake well. Pour over pasta and vegetable mixture. Mix well.

Serves 8.

wild rice and cranberry salad

Nutrition notes:
Because brown rice is unpolished and contains the germ and bran of the grain, it provides more fibre and B vitamins than polished white rice. Wild rice also adds texture and flavour to this salad, as well as fibre, folic acid and other B vitamins.

Nutritional analysis per serving:
194 calories
4 g protein
6 g fat
1 g saturated fat
32 g carbohydrate
0 mg cholesterol
91 mg sodium
3 g fibre

This scrumptious salad is crunchy and full of flavour. Try pine nuts in place of almonds, and chopped dried apricots for the cranberries.

2 cups	cooked wild rice	475 mL
2 cups	cooked brown rice	475 mL
1	stalk celery, diced	1
$1/4$ cup	slivered almonds, toasted	60 mL
$1/2$ cup	dried cranberries	120 mL
$1/4$ cup	thinly sliced green onions	60 mL
$1/2$ cup	orange juice	120 mL
2 Tbsp	olive oil	30 mL
$1/2$ tsp	dry mustard	2.5 mL
$1/4$ tsp	salt	1.2 mL
$1/8$ tsp	ground black pepper	.5 mL
2 tsp	sugar	10 mL

Mix together wild rice, brown rice, celery, almonds, cranberries and green onions in bowl. In small bowl, combine orange juice, oil, mustard, salt, pepper and sugar. Stir until sugar is dissolved. Pour over rice mixture. Mix well. Serve cold.

Serves 8.

butternut squash risotto

Nutrition notes:
Of all the rice available,
brown rice is the highest
in fibre and nutrients. For
variety, though, rice such
as jasmine, basmati and
Arborio can be part of a
healthy diet.

**Nutritional analysis
per serving:**
408 calories
9 g protein
6 g fat
1 g saturated fat
78 g carbohydrate
3 mg cholesterol
379 mg sodium
8 g fibre

Arborio rice with its short, fat grain and higher starch content is traditionally used for risotto. For an authentic touch, serve risotto in painted Italian pasta bowls. Add grilled vegetables on the side and a wedge of focaccia bread.

3 cups	peeled butternut squash, cut in bite-sized cubes	720 mL
1	10-oz (284-mL) can chicken broth	1
4 cups	water	950 mL
1 Tbsp	olive oil	15 mL
1	small onion, finely diced	1
1	clove garlic, minced	1
1^1/2 cups	Arborio rice	360 mL
^{1}/3 cup	dry white wine	80 mL
^{1}/4 tsp	freshly ground black pepper	1.2 mL
3 Tbsp	grated Parmesan cheese	45 mL

Steam squash until tender but still firm, about 10 minutes. Set aside.

In covered pot, bring broth and water to a boil, and allow to simmer. Meanwhile, heat oil in another pot over medium heat. Add onion and sauté until golden. Add garlic and sauté 1 minute. Add rice and sauté, while stirring, about 1–2 minutes. Add wine and stir until wine has evaporated. Add ^{1}/2 cup (120 mL) of simmering broth, stirring continually. When liquid has been absorbed, add another ^{1}/2 cup (120 mL) of simmering broth. Continue to add broth ^{1}/2 cup (120 mL) at a time until rice is tender but still firm. This will take about 20 minutes. You may not need all the liquid.

Stir in squash. Season with pepper and heat through. Stir in Parmesan cheese. Serve immediately.

Serves 4.

cilantro rice

Nutrition notes:
Fresh herbs are a delightful fat-free way to flavour foods, especially when they are fresh from the garden. Keep a flowerpot of fresh herbs on the windowsill for a year-round source of herbs.

Nutritional analysis per serving:
207 calories
5 g protein
2 g fat
0 g saturated fat
40 g carbohydrate
0 mg cholesterol
225 mg sodium
1 g fibre

This is an excellent side dish to serve with chicken fajitas. The jalapeño peppers add a zip, but are removed before serving—unless, of course, you are adventurous!

1 Tbsp	olive oil	15 mL
1	onion, finely chopped	1
2	cloves garlic, minced	2
2 cups	long-grain white rice	475 mL
1	10-oz (284-mL) can chicken broth	1
1 3/4 cups	water	420 mL
1	bunch fresh cilantro, washed	1
3	jalapeño peppers	3

Heat oil in deep-sided sauté pan over medium heat. Add onion and cook until soft, about 5 minutes. Add garlic and cook 1 minute. Add rice and sauté until rice is coated. Add broth and water, and bring to a boil. Place cilantro in middle of pan and arrange jalapeño peppers around cilantro.

Cover and reduce heat to simmer. Cook until all liquid has been absorbed and rice is tender. Remove peppers and cilantro before serving rice.

Serves 8.

Timesaver tip:
For a simple flavoured rice dish, add a chicken bouillon cube to the cooking water. Add chopped parsley before serving.

rice and bean salad

Nutrition notes:
Beans, rice and vegetables are 3 of the food groups in Canada's Food Guide for Healthy Eating. A balanced diet means eating appropriate servings from all food groups each day. Try to eat food from at least 3 of the 4 food groups at each meal.

Nutritional analysis per serving:
152 calories
5 g protein
2 g fat
0 g saturated fat
29 g carbohydrate
0 mg cholesterol
268 mg sodium
4 g fibre

Roasted peppers have a sweet mellow flavour that is enhanced by the balsamic vinegar and olive oil dressing. The various contrasts in texture also make this salad interesting.

1	red bell pepper	1
1	yellow bell pepper	1
3 cups	cooked basmati rice	720 mL
1	19-oz (540-mL) can black beans, drained and rinsed	1
1	12-oz (340-mL) can corn niblets, drained	1
4 cups	chopped romaine lettuce	950 mL
1/4 cup	chopped parsley	60 mL
1/4 cup	chopped green onions	60 mL
3 Tbsp	balsamic vinegar	45 mL
1 1/2 Tbsp	olive oil	22.5 mL
1 Tbsp	sugar	15 mL
1	clove garlic, crushed and finely chopped	1
1/4 tsp	salt	1.2 mL
1/8 tsp	ground black pepper	.5 mL

Preheat oven to 375°F (190°C). Place whole bell peppers on baking sheet and roast in oven until peppers are slightly darkened and skin is blistered, about 45 minutes. Cool slightly and peel. Slice into thin strips.

In large bowl, combine peppers, rice, beans, corn, lettuce, parsley and green onions. Set aside. In small bowl, whisk together vinegar, oil, sugar, garlic, salt and pepper. Add to rice mixture and mix in gently.

Serves 12.

barley pilaf

Nutrition notes:
The folic acid, other
B vitamins and soluble
fibre in barley make it an
especially heart-healthy
food.

**Nutritional analysis
per serving:**
175 calories
5 g protein
4 g fat
0 g saturated fat
29 g carbohydrate
0 mg cholesterol
373 mg sodium
6 g fibre

Barley is a nice change from the usual potatoes or rice. This delicious combo can be served as a side dish or a light entrée, and is just as good the next day. Make a double batch and reheat leftovers.

1 Tbsp	oil	15 mL
1	carrot, diced	1
1	stalk celery, diced	1
1	green onion, chopped	1
1	clove garlic, crushed	1
1	10-oz (284-mL) can corn, drained	1
1 tsp	dried thyme	5 mL
1^1/$_2$ cups	chicken broth	360 mL
^{1}/$_2$ cup	white wine	120 mL
^{1}/$_4$ cup	chopped fresh parsley	60 mL
^{3}/$_4$ cup	pot barley	180 mL
^{1}/$_4$ cup	frozen peas	60 mL

Heat oil in medium pot over medium heat and sauté carrots, celery, green onion and garlic for 5 minutes. Add corn, thyme, broth, wine, parsley and pot barley. Bring to a boil.

Reduce heat, cover and simmer for about 1–1^1/$_2$ hours, or until barley is soft. Add peas just before serving and heat through.

Serves 6 as a side dish.

Timesaver tip:
This is just as good the next day, so make a double batch and reheat the leftovers.

spinach and lemon rice

Nutrition notes:
Popeye had it right!
Spinach is a power-packed vegetable full of all kinds of phyto-chemicals, vitamins and minerals. Add it to salads or soups whenever the recipe calls for leafy greens.

Nutritional analysis per serving:
236 calories
8 g protein
6 g fat
1 g saturated fat
41 g carbohydrate
1 mg cholesterol
332 mg sodium
6 g fibre

This traditional, rustic recipe is delicious both hot and cold. The final squeeze of lemon juice is the secret to the dish. The end result is a softer rice than you may expect, but that is exactly the way it should turn out!

2 Tbsp	olive oil	30 mL
2	medium onions, finely chopped	2
1	clove garlic, minced	1
1	bay leaf	1
	salt and ground black pepper to taste	
1 cup	long-grain white rice	240 mL
3 Tbsp	tomato paste	45 mL
2 lbs	fresh spinach, washed, dried, stems removed	900 g
1 1/2 cups	beef broth	360 mL
	juice of 1 lemon	

Heat oil in large saucepan over medium heat. Add onions and sauté until soft and slightly golden. Add garlic, bay leaf, salt and pepper and cook for 1 minute. Add rice and tomato paste, and stir until blended. Add spinach and mix well. Stir in beef broth. Cover and bring to a boil.

Reduce heat and simmer for 25 minutes, or until rice is cooked. Remove from heat and squeeze lemon juice over rice mixture just before serving.

Serves 6.

Timesaver tip:
Bunch spinach is often very dirty and time-consuming to wash. Prewashed, trimmed spinach in a bag is just as nutritious but much less work.

couscous with mushrooms

Nutrition notes:
Whether it is rice, wheat or couscous, the whole-grain version provides more fibre and phytosterols than the refined white product. Look for whole-grain couscous when you shop.

Nutritional analysis per serving:
203 calories
8 g protein
2 g fat
0 g saturated fat
38 g carbohydrate
0 mg cholesterol
264 mg sodium
3 g fibre

Keep couscous on hand for days when you really have no time to boil potatoes or steam rice. It's ready to eat 5 minutes after the stock has boiled. Any type of mushroom is fine in this dish, but for a gourmet touch, use varieties such as oyster or shiitake. Serve with baked salmon and stir-fried greens for a quick dinner.

1 tsp	oil	5 mL
1	small onion, chopped	1
1 cup	sliced mushrooms	240 mL
2 cups	chicken broth	475 mL
1¹/₂ cups	couscous	360 mL

Heat oil over medium heat in saucepan. Add onion and sauté until slightly browned. Add mushrooms and sauté until mushrooms are softened. Add chicken broth and bring to a boil. Remove from heat. Mix in couscous. Cover and let stand for 5 minutes. Stir and fluff up with a fork.

Serves 6.

Timesaver tip:
For a very simple couscous dish, boil 2 cups (475 mL) of water in a pot, add a chicken or vegetable bouillon cube and stir until dissolved. Mix in 1¹/₂ cups (360 mL) couscous, cover and let stand for 5 minutes. Fluff with a fork and serve.

oven-baked stuffing

Nutrition notes:
About $^1/_3$ of the fat
in poultry is saturated.
Cooking the stuffing
separately helps to
keep saturated fat
content down.

**Nutritional analysis
per serving:**
150 calories
5 g protein
5 g fat
1 g saturated fat
22 g carbohydrate
18 mg cholesterol
531 mg sodium
1 g fibre

Turkey cooks faster and remains just as moist when the stuffing is cooked separately. Put one or two quartered onions, lemon halves and a few sprigs of sage or rosemary in the bird cavity to add flavour.

2 Tbsp	margarine	30 mL
$^1/_2$	medium onion, chopped	$^1/_2$
2	stalks celery, chopped	2
1 cup	sliced mushrooms	240 mL
$^1/_2$ tsp	salt	2.5 mL
$^1/_4$ tsp	ground black pepper	1.2 mL
$^3/_4$ lb	dry bread cubes or strips, about 8 cups (2 L)	340 g
1	egg	1
$2^1/_2$ cups	chicken broth	600 mL
1 Tbsp	poultry seasoning	15 mL
$^1/_4$ cup	water	60 mL

Preheat oven to 350°F (175°C). Melt margarine in frying pan over medium heat. Add onion, celery, mushrooms, salt and pepper. Sauté until vegetables are softened. Place bread in large bowl and add onion mixture. Whisk together egg, chicken broth, poultry seasoning and water. Add to bread cubes and mix well until bread is moistened.

Spread evenly in greased 9- x 9-in (23- x 23-cm) baking dish. Bake covered for 45 minutes, or until lightly browned and pulling away from side of dish.

Serves 12.

Timesaver tip:
An unstuffed turkey takes less time to cook than one with stuffing. Cook the stuffing in the oven while you are carving the turkey, or cook it ahead of time and microwave it before serving.

main courses

beef and tofu stir-fry

Nutrition notes:
Using a combination of beef and tofu allows for plenty of protein and flavour, but has just half the saturated fat and cholesterol of beef alone.

Nutritional analysis per serving:
314 calories
31 g protein
14 g fat
2 g saturated fat
16 g carbohydrate
26 mg cholesterol
681 mg sodium
6 g fibre

This tastes great even without the beef for a vegetarian meal. For more spice, add extra ginger and a pinch of pepper. Serve over jasmine rice.

¹/₂ lb	lean sirloin tip beef, thinly sliced	225 g
2 Tbsp	scotch whiskey	30 mL
1 Tbsp	soy sauce	15 mL
1 tsp	minced fresh ginger	5 mL
1 Tbsp	soy sauce	15 mL
1 Tbsp	oyster sauce	15 mL
1 Tbsp	cornstarch	15 mL
1 Tbsp	oil	15 mL
1 lb	broccoli florets	450 g
1	carrot, thinly sliced	1
1 Tbsp	sliced fresh ginger	15 mL
¹/₄ cup	water	60 mL
2 cups	mushrooms, quartered	475 mL
1	12-oz (340-g) pkg firm tofu, cubed	1

Marinate beef in whiskey, 1 Tbsp (15 mL) soy sauce and 1 tsp (5 mL) minced ginger for at least ¹/₂ hour.

Mix together remaining 1 Tbsp. (15 mL) soy sauce, oyster sauce and cornstarch. Set aside.

Heat 1 tsp (5 mL) of the oil in wok over medium heat. Sear beef for about 1 minute. Remove from wok and set aside. Heat remaining 2 tsp (10 mL) oil in wok. Add broccoli, carrot, ginger and half of the water. Cook for 2 minutes. Add additional water if necessary. Add mushrooms, tofu and beef. Add cornstarch mixture and stir well. Cover and cook until vegetables are tender and sauce is thickened and clear.

Serves 4.

marinated beef brochettes

Nutrition notes:
Because much of the fat in beef is the saturated type, buying lean beef and trimming visible fat is important.

Nutritional analysis per serving:
214 calories
26 g protein
6 g fat
2 g saturated fat
11 g carbohydrate
55 mg cholesterol
416 mg sodium
0 g fibre

Let the beef marinate overnight for the most flavour. For a festive meal, arrange vegetables, such as cut-up red peppers, mushrooms and onion wedges, with the beef on long skewers. Baste with sauce while cooking. If you are using bamboo skewers, soak them in water for 30 minutes before using them.

1$^1/_2$ lbs	lean beef, such as sirloin tip or inside round	680 g
$^1/_4$ cup	sodium-reduced soy sauce	60 mL
$^1/_4$ cup	white wine	60 mL
$^1/_4$ cup	brown sugar	60 mL
1	1-in (2.5-cm) knob fresh ginger, sliced	1
2	cloves garlic, crushed	2
1	green onion, sliced	1

Cut beef into 1-in (2.5-cm) cubes. Combine remaining ingredients and pour over beef. Stir until beef is coated. Cover and put in refrigerator to marinate for 2–24 hours.

Using bamboo or metal skewers, put 3–4 cubes of beef on each skewer. Broil or barbecue beef for 5–10 minutes, or to desired doneness.

Serves 6.

Timesaver tip:
Buy small sirloin steaks and marinate them in the sauce overnight. Barbecue or broil the steaks rather than make brochettes.

oven-braised beef in red wine sauce

Nutrition notes:
Eye of the round is one of the leanest cuts of red meat available. Small portions of lean red meat can be part of a heart-healthy diet.

Nutritional analysis per serving:
240 calories
24 g protein
10 g fat
4 g saturated fat
6 g carbohydrate
65 mg cholesterol
148 mg sodium
0 g fibre

Cooking beef in red wine tenderizes and flavours the meat, and gives the sauce a rich mellow taste.

2 lbs	eye of the round beef roast	900 g
4	cloves garlic, sliced	4
1 cup	red wine	240 mL
	hot water	
1	beef bouillon cube	1
$^1/_4$ cup	flour	60 mL
1 tsp	oil	5 mL
1	large white onion, sliced	1
	sprig sage or rosemary	

Preheat oven to 325°F (165°C). Make about 8 small slits in roast. Put garlic slice in each slit. Sprinkle remaining garlic in roasting pan. Place roast in roasting pan and pour wine over. Cover and roast for about 2 hours, or until meat is very tender. Remove meat from pan and set aside.

Pour liquid from pan into measuring cup and remove all fat. Add hot water to make 2$^1/_4$ cups (535 mL) liquid. Pour into medium bowl. Add bouillon cube and mix until dissolved. Whisk flour into sauce until no lumps remain.

Heat oil in sauté pan, add onion and sauté until soft. Whisk sauce mixture once more and pour over onion, mixing constantly. Cook over medium-low heat until thickened to gravy consistency. Cook 5 minutes more, whisking frequently. Meanwhile, slice meat into thin slices. Place meat gently in pan, cover with sauce and heat through. Arrange meat on serving platter. Pour sauce over top. Garnish with sprig of sage or rosemary.

Serves 8.

rosemary lamb stew

Nutrition notes:
Cuts of meat that are away from the bone tend to be leaner than others. Good choices for beef are sirloin, rump, round or flank. Leg of lamb is also a lean choice—just remember to trim off any visible fat before cooking.

Nutritional analysis per serving:
506 calories
38 g protein
14 g fat
4 g saturated fat
49 g carbohydrate
104 mg cholesterol
516 mg sodium
5 g fibre

A classic combination of lamb and rosemary with red wine gives this stew a Mediterranean touch.

1 Tbsp	olive oil	15 mL
1 lb	boneless leg of lamb, trimmed and cubed	450 g
3	cloves garlic, minced	3
$1/2$ cup	red wine	120 mL
1	28-oz (796-mL) can plum tomatoes, cut up, with juice	1
1 Tbsp	fresh rosemary	15 mL
$1/4$ tsp	red pepper flakes (optional)	1.2 mL
3 cups	halved nugget potatoes	720 mL
1 cup	quartered mushrooms	240 mL
	salt and ground black pepper to taste	

Heat oil in large sauté pan over high heat. When oil is hot, add meat. Reduce heat to medium and brown meat on all sides. Add garlic and red wine and cook for 5 minutes. Add tomatoes, rosemary and red pepper flakes, if desired. Cover pan and simmer for 1 hour. Stir occasionally to prevent sticking. Add water if additional liquid is needed.

Add the potatoes and mushrooms. Cover and simmer for $1/2$ hour, or until potatoes are tender. Stir occasionally to prevent sticking. Season to taste with salt and pepper.

Serves 4.

moose stew

Nutrition notes:
Wild game, such as moose, deer and rabbit, is a good, lean protein choice. But remember, a serving size for meat is still 3 oz (85 g), or the size of a deck of cards.

Nutritional analysis per serving:
420 calories
26 g protein
5 g fat
1 g saturated fat
70 g carbohydrate
50 mg cholesterol
626 mg sodium
9 g fibre

If wild game is not available, lean stewing beef is an excellent substitute. Add Brussels sprouts, beets or sweet potato for variety.

$^1/_4$ cup	flour	60 mL
$^1/_2$ tsp	salt	2.5 mL
$^1/_2$ tsp	ground black pepper	2.5 mL
$^3/_4$ lb	moose meat, trimmed and cubed	340 g
1 Tbsp	olive oil	15 mL
1	beef bouillon cube	1
4 cups	water	950 mL
2	cloves garlic, minced	2
5	sun-dried tomatoes (not oil-packed)	5
2	carrots, cut into 1-in (2.5-cm) pieces	2
12	nugget potatoes	12
1	medium parsnip, peeled and cut into rounds	1
1	small onion, sliced	1
1	small turnip, peeled and cubed	1
$^1/_2$ tsp	each dried basil and dried oregano	2.5 mL
1	medium yam, peeled and cubed	1
1	stalk celery, diced	1
2 Tbsp	coarsely chopped fresh parsley	30 mL

Put flour, salt and pepper in plastic bag large enough to hold meat. Add meat and shake well until meat is coated with flour mixture. Heat oil in large pot over medium-high heat. Add meat and cook until browned, taking care not to burn.

Dissolve bouillon cube in 1 cup (240 mL) boiling water. Top water up to 4 cups (950 mL) and add to meat mixture. Add garlic.

Cover and simmer over low heat for 2 hours, adding water if necessary.

Pour boiling water over sun-dried tomatoes and let sit for 10 minutes. Drain tomatoes and cut lengthwise into strips. Add carrots, potatoes, parsnip, onion, turnip, sun-dried tomatoes, basil and oregano to meat mixture. Cover and simmer for 20 minutes. Add yam and celery and cook for additional 10 minutes, or until all vegetables are cooked through. Add parsley just before serving.

Serves 4.

sweet and sour pineapple pork tenderloin

Nutrition notes:
Pork tenderloin is lean
and low in saturated fats
compared to most other
cuts of meat. Lean meats
are great sources of
protein, iron, zinc and
B vitamins. Be sure to
keep portions down to
the size of your palm to
limit extra calories and
cholesterol.

**Nutritional analysis
per serving:**
349 calories
27 g protein
7 g fat
1 g saturated fat
47 g carbohydrate
64 mg cholesterol
386 mg sodium
4 g fibre

The sweet and sour sauce in this recipe is also great with chicken or tofu. Use firm or medium-firm tofu cubes, and stir them in gently when the thickened sauce is simmering with the vegetables. The amount of sugar can be reduced to 2 Tbsp (30 mL) if you prefer a tarter flavour. Serve with rice.

$^1/_2$ cup	water	120 mL
2 Tbsp	ketchup	30 mL
$^1/_4$ cup	vinegar	60 mL
2 Tbsp	cornstarch	30 mL
$^1/_4$ cup	brown sugar	60 mL
1 Tbsp	sodium-reduced soy sauce	15 mL
1	14-oz (398-mL) can pineapple tidbits in its own juice, drained (reserve juice, about $^3/_4$ cup/180 mL)	1
1 Tbsp	canola oil	15 mL
1 lb	lean pork tenderloin, cut into 1-in (2.5-cm) cubes	450 g
2	cloves garlic, crushed	2
1	medium onion, cut into 16 wedges	1
4	stalks celery, sliced diagonally in $^1/_2$-in (1.2-cm) pieces	4
1	medium red bell pepper, cut into small chunks	1
$^3/_4$ cup	snow peas	180 mL

Combine water, ketchup, vinegar, cornstarch, brown sugar, soy sauce and reserved pineapple juice in bowl. Set aside.

Heat oil in large sauté pan or wok over medium heat. Add pork cubes and garlic and sauté until pork is lightly browned, about 5 minutes. Add onion, celery and red pepper, and stir-fry for 3 minutes. Add pineapple tidbits.

Stir cornstarch mixture once more, and add to pan. Stir constantly until sauce thickens. Let simmer for 5–6 minutes. Add snow peas and cook 1 minute. Serve immediately.

Serves 4.

Timesaver tip:
Sweet and sour sauce is available ready-made at the supermarket, and can be used to flavour meats such as pork. However, this recipe really is very quick if your vegetables are precut.

roast pork tenderloin with sour cherries

Nutrition notes:
Traditional gravies, béarnaise and hollandaise sauces are high in saturated fats. Fruit sauces, such as cranberry, chutney, mint jelly and salsas are good substitutes, adding flavour to meats with minimal added fat. Jars of sour cherries in light syrup are available in the canned fruit section at the supermarket.

Nutritional analysis per serving:
220 calories
25 g protein
5 g fat
1 g saturated fat
17 g carbohydrate
64 mg cholesterol
187 mg sodium
1 g fibre

Add wild rice and steamed asparagus for a simple yet elegant meal.

2 Tbsp	Dijon mustard	30 mL
$1/4$ cup	balsamic vinegar	60 mL
1 Tbsp	honey	15 mL
1 Tbsp	olive oil	15 mL
$1/4$ tsp	salt	1.2 mL
$1/8$ tsp	ground black pepper	.5 mL
3	cloves garlic, crushed	3
$1^1/2$ lbs	pork tenderloin	680 g
1 cup	sour cherries, canned in light syrup, drained (reserve $1/2$ cup/120 mL of juice)	240 mL
$1^1/2$ tsp	cornstarch	7.5 mL

To make marinade, whisk together mustard, vinegar, honey, oil, salt, pepper and garlic. Prick pork tenderloin all over with fork to allow marinade to be absorbed. Pour marinade over pork, cover, and marinate in refrigerator for 2–24 hours. Turn the pork from time to time to make sure all sides are marinated.

Preheat oven to 350°F (175°C). Place marinated pork tenderloin in shallow roasting pan and bake for 45 minutes or until done.

Slice pork into $1/4$-in-thick (.6-cm) slices and arrange on serving platter. Sprinkle with sour cherries. Place cornstarch and reserved cherry juice in small pot and whisk to remove any lumps. Cook over low heat until thickened. Pour over pork and cherries.

Serves 6.

chicken with corn and black beans

Nutritional analysis per serving:
315 calories
32 g protein
8 g fat
1 g saturated fat
25 g carbohydrate
72 mg cholesterol
1172 mg sodium
7 g fibre

For a change, turn this recipe into a wrap. Slice the cooked chicken and place it in the middle of a flour tortilla. Add the bean mixture and a little fat-free sour cream. Roll up the tortilla and it's a wrap!

1 cup	canned black beans, rinsed	240 mL
1	14-oz (398-mL) can corn niblets	1
3/4 cup	salsa	180 mL
1	small red bell pepper, chopped	1
4	boneless, skinless chicken breast halves	4
1 tsp	ground cumin	5 mL
1/2 tsp	garlic powder	2.5 mL
1/2 tsp	salt	2.5 mL
2 tsp	canola oil	10 mL
3 Tbsp	chopped fresh cilantro	45 mL

Combine black beans, corn, salsa and red pepper. Set aside.

Sprinkle chicken with cumin, garlic powder and salt. Heat oil in large non-stick skillet over medium-high heat. Add chicken and cook for 4 minutes, turning to brown both sides of chicken. Spread black bean mixture on top of chicken and simmer covered over low heat for 10 minutes, or until chicken is cooked. Remove chicken and set aside.

Continue to cook bean mixture uncovered over medium heat for 3 minutes, stirring frequently. Place chicken on serving plates, top with bean mixture and sprinkle with cilantro.

Serves 4.

chicken pilaf

Nutrition notes:
Whenever you can, use brown rice for its extra fibre and nutrients. Just remember that brown rice takes longer to cook than white rice. White rice takes about 25 minutes to cook; brown rice may take as much as 45 minutes.

Nutritional analysis per serving:
524 calories
34 g protein
8 g fat
2 g saturated fat
78 g carbohydrate
72 mg cholesterol
1028 mg sodium
5 g fibre

A "one-pot wonder" meal! Make a salad and then relax while the pilaf cooks.

1	frying chicken	1
1 Tbsp	oil	15 mL
1	large carrot, diced	1
2	stalks celery, diced	2
1	small onion, chopped	1
1	clove garlic, minced	1
1	14-oz (398-mL) can stewed tomatoes	1
2 Tbsp	barbecue sauce	30 mL
$1/4$ tsp	cayenne pepper (optional)	1.2 mL
$1/2$ tsp	coarsely ground black pepper	2.5 mL
3 cups	tomato or vegetable juice	720 mL
$1^1/2$ cups	long-grain rice	360 mL

Cut chicken into small serving pieces and remove skin. Heat oil in large heavy pot over medium-high heat. Add chicken and brown on all sides. Add carrot, celery and onion. Cook until onion is softened. Add garlic, tomatoes, barbecue sauce, cayenne and black pepper, juice and rice. Mix well. Bring to a boil, stirring often.

Turn heat to low, cover and simmer, stirring occasionally, for 45 minutes, or until chicken and rice are cooked.

Serves 4.

Timesaver tip:
For just a little less hassle, use 4 boneless skinless breast halves instead of a whole chicken. Cut each breast half into 2 or 3 pieces.

pineapple baked chicken

Nutrition notes:
When cooking chicken in a sauce, remove the skin before cooking. If the chicken is barbecued, broiled or roasted and the fat is allowed to drip off, cook the chicken with the skin on, but be sure to remove it before eating the chicken.

Nutritional analysis per serving:
259 calories
28 g protein
4 g fat
1 g saturated fat
27 g carbohydrate
72 mg cholesterol
89 mg sodium
3 g fibre

The long cooking time makes the chicken very tender as it absorbs the pineapple flavour.

4	chicken breast halves, skin removed	4
4	cloves garlic, sliced salt to taste	4
1	onion, sliced	1
1	red bell pepper, sliced	1
2	stalks celery, sliced diagonally into $1/2$-in (1.2-cm) pieces	2
1	19-oz (540-mL) can unsweetened pineapple tidbits (reserve juice)	1
2 Tbsp	flour	30 mL
$1/4$ cup	water	60 mL
2 Tbsp	brown sugar	30 mL

Preheat oven to 375°F (190°C). Place chicken in roasting pan. Add garlic and sprinkle with salt. Add onion, red pepper and celery. Pour reserved pineapple juice over chicken. Cover and bake for 75 minutes. Remove chicken from pan and keep warm in serving dish. Remove vegetables from pan and set aside.

Place roasting pan with remaining liquid on stovetop over medium heat. Whisk flour and water together. Stir flour mixture into pan juices. Cook and stir over medium heat until thickened. Add sugar, pineapple tidbits and vegetables. Heat thoroughly and serve over chicken.

Serves 4.

Timesaver tip:
Cook chicken with purchased sweet and sour sauce. Add pineapple chunks, if desired.

stir-fried chicken with fresh tomatoes

Nutritional analysis per serving:
184 calories
16 g protein
4 g fat
1 g saturated fat
22 g carbohydrate
36 mg cholesterol
393 mg sodium
3 g fibre

This delicious stir-fry can be made in 30 minutes—cut up all the vegetables while the chicken is marinating. Use Roma tomatoes, which hold their shape. For more colour, add green peppers. Serve over rice.

To marinate chicken:

2	boneless, skinless chicken breast halves	2
2 tsp	soy sauce	10 mL
1 tsp	sugar	5 mL
2 tsp	brandy	10 mL
2 tsp	fresh ginger, thinly slivered	10 mL
$^1/_4$ tsp	ground black pepper	1.2 mL
1 Tbsp	cornstarch	15 mL

Cut chicken breasts into 2- x $^1/_2$-in (5- x 1.2-cm) strips. Combine remaining ingredients and pour over chicken. Mix well and refrigerate for 15 minutes or up to 8 hours.

To assemble dish:

1 tsp	canola oil	5 mL
$1^1/_2$	white onions, cut into thin wedges	$1^1/_2$
5	tomatoes, each cut into 8 wedges	5
2	cloves garlic, crushed	2
2 tsp	vinegar	10 mL
4 tsp	sugar	20 mL
2 tsp	soy sauce	10 mL
2 tsp	cornstarch	10 mL
$^1/_4$ cup	water	60 mL
1	green onion, cut into 1-in (2.5-cm) lengths	1

Heat oil in non-stick wok over medium heat. Add chicken and marinade and cook until chicken is cooked through, about 5 minutes. Remove chicken from wok and set aside. In the same wok, sauté onion wedges for a few minutes, or until just tender. Remove onion from wok and set aside.

Add tomatoes and garlic and sauté for 1 minute. Combine vinegar, sugar, soy sauce, cornstarch and water. Mix well. Add mixture to wok and heat just until thickened, mixing gently. Add chicken, onion wedges and green onion. Heat thoroughly.

Serves 4.

Timesaver tip:
Cut up the vegetables the night before and marinate the meat overnight, for a super-quick meal the next day. Be sure to put the rice on to cook before starting the stir-fry.

chicken and nectarine stir-fry

Nutrition notes:
It is not just oranges and other citrus fruits that are high in vitamin C. Most fruits and vegetables are excellent sources of vitamin C and other antioxidants.

Nutritional analysis per serving:
252 calories
28 g protein
7 g fat
1 g saturated fat
18 g carbohydrate
72 mg cholesterol
507 mg sodium
3 g fibre

Nectarines and chicken may seem unusual, but it's a tasty combination. Don't overcook the nectarines, to retain their fresh flavour and texture. You can also use drained canned peach slices instead of nectarines.

3	boneless, skinless chicken breast halves (about $^3/_4$ lb/340 g)	3
1 Tbsp	soy sauce	15 mL
$^1/_4$ tsp	salt	1.2 mL
2 tsp	cornstarch	10 mL
1 Tbsp	cider vinegar	15 mL
1 Tbsp	ketchup	15 mL
1 Tbsp	sugar	15 mL
2 Tbsp	water	30 mL
1 Tbsp	canola oil	15 mL
1	green bell pepper, sliced	1
1	red bell pepper, sliced	1
1 Tbsp	minced fresh ginger	15 mL
1	clove garlic, minced	1
$^1/_2$	medium onion, sliced	$^1/_2$
3	nectarines, peeled and sliced into eighths	3

Slice chicken into $^1/_2$-in-wide (1.2-cm) strips and place in bowl. Mix soy sauce, salt and cornstarch. Combine with chicken. Set aside for 30 minutes.

In small bowl, combine cider vinegar, ketchup, sugar and water. Mix and set aside.

In non-stick pan or wok, heat oil over medium heat. Add chicken and stir-fry for 5 minutes, or until chicken is just opaque. Add peppers, ginger, garlic and onion. Stir-fry for 2 minutes, until vegetables are tender-crisp. Add vinegar mixture.

Stir-fry until sauce is slightly thickened, about 1 minute. Add nectarines and cook just until nectarines are heated through.

Serves 4.

chicken à l'orange

Nutrition notes:
A glass of calcium-fortified orange juice provides the same amount of calcium as one glass of milk. Keep in mind, though, that too many glasses of any juice can add up to a lot of extra calories.

Nutritional analysis per serving:
243 calories
27 g protein
8 g fat
2 g saturated fat
14 g carbohydrate
72 mg cholesterol
69 mg sodium
1 g fibre

This chicken dish with orange sauce is delicious served over jasmine rice along with steamed greens. For a change of flavour, try pineapple juice instead of orange juice.

1$^1/_2$ cups	orange juice	360 mL
3 Tbsp	brown sugar	45 mL
2 Tbsp	olive oil	30 mL
6	3-oz (85-g) boneless, skinless chicken breast halves	6
2	cloves garlic, crushed	2
1	medium onion, sliced into thin rounds	1

Mix juice and sugar together and set aside. Heat oil in non-stick frying pan over medium heat. Place chicken in pan and sauté until golden brown. Turn chicken over and add garlic and onion. Sauté until onion is translucent. Add orange juice mixture. Bring to a boil. Reduce heat, cover and simmer for 30 minutes, or until chicken is tender. Turn chicken pieces over halfway through cooking.

Serves 6.

mediterranean chicken

Serve over bow-tie pasta with pan-seared asparagus and a tossed salad. If you prefer white meat, use boneless skinless chicken breasts instead of thighs.

Nutrition notes:
Chicken thighs are higher in fat than breasts, but are more economical. Make sure you remove the skin and trim off all the visible fat before cooking.

Nutritional analysis per serving:
187 calories
15 g protein
8 g fat
2 g saturated fat
9 g carbohydrate
50 mg cholesterol
485 mg sodium
2 g fibre

8	chicken thighs, skin removed and fat trimmed	8
2 Tbsp	flour	30 mL
1 Tbsp	olive oil	15 mL
1	medium onion, chopped	1
2	cloves garlic, crushed	2
$1/2$ cup	red wine	120 mL
2 Tbsp	balsamic vinegar	30 mL
1	28-oz (796-mL) can tomatoes, mashed with a fork	1
$1/3$ cup	kalamata olives, pitted and sliced	80 mL
2 Tbsp	capers, rinsed	30 mL
	pinch red pepper flakes	
	fresh basil	

Coat chicken with flour. Heat oil in large frying pan over medium heat. Sauté chicken until browned on all sides. Remove chicken and set aside.

Add onion to pan and cook until soft. Add garlic and sauté 1 minute. Add wine, vinegar, tomatoes, olives, capers, pepper flakes and chicken. Cover and simmer for $1/2$ hour, or until chicken is cooked. Tear basil into small pieces and sprinkle over chicken just before serving.

Serves 8.

Timesaver tip:
Pour ready-made chunky spaghetti sauce over browned chicken. Sprinkle with sliced olives and capers. Simmer until chicken is cooked through.

rotini with chicken and snow peas

Nutritional analysis per serving:
604 calories
32 g protein
8 g fat
1 g saturated fat
91 g carbohydrate
37 mg cholesterol
707 mg sodium
3 g fibre

Brandy gives this recipe a rich flavour, but you can use chicken broth instead. Serve with a sprinkle of grated low-fat Parmesan cheese, if desired.

1 Tbsp	oil	15 mL
1/2 cup	sliced onion	120 mL
1/4 cup	sun-dried tomatoes (not oil-packed), soaked and diced	60 mL
4	cloves garlic, minced	4
1/2 tsp	salt	2.5 mL
1/4 tsp	ground black pepper	1.2 mL
2	boneless, skinless chicken breast halves	2
1/4 cup	brandy	60 mL
1 cup	skim milk	240 mL
1	large tomato, chopped	1
1 lb	snow peas	450 g
1/4 cup	fresh basil	60 mL
3/4 lb	dried rotini, cooked	340 g
3 Tbsp	balsamic vinegar	45 mL

Heat oil in sauté pan over medium heat. Add onion, sun-dried tomatoes, garlic, salt and pepper. Stir-fry for 5 minutes. Cut chicken into bite-sized pieces and add to pan. Stir-fry for 5 minutes, until chicken is cooked. Add brandy and cook for 2 minutes. Add skim milk and bring to a boil. Add tomato, snow peas, basil and cooked pasta. Cook for 2 minutes, until snow peas are bright green and pasta is hot. Add balsamic vinegar and mix well.

Serves 4.

Timesaver tip:
Replace the chicken with 12 oz (340 g) firm tofu, cut in large dice. Use whatever vegetables you have on hand.

sweet and sour turkey meatballs

Nutrition notes:
For the leanest ground turkey, cut skinless turkey breast into 1-in (2.5-cm) cubes and grind it up yourself in the food processor.

Nutritional analysis per serving:
331 calories
21 g protein
11 g fat
3 g saturated fat
39 g carbohydrate
89 mg cholesterol
188 mg sodium
2 g fibre

Serve these fruity meatballs with whole-grain rice and sautéed greens. Use extra-lean ground beef or ground chicken in place of the turkey if you prefer.

6	prunes	6
6	dried apricots	6
1 lb	ground turkey breast	450 g
1/2 cup	chopped parsley	120 mL
1/4 tsp	salt	1.2 mL
1/8 tsp	ground black pepper	.5 mL
1 tsp	oil	5 mL
1	small onion, chopped	1
1/3 cup	tomato paste	80 mL
	juice of 1 lemon	
1/4 cup	brown sugar	60 mL
2 Tbsp	raisins	30 mL
1 1/4 cups	water	300 mL

Soak prunes and apricots in hot water for 10 minutes. Drain. Cut each piece in half. Set aside.

Mix turkey, parsley, salt and pepper in bowl. Set aside.

Heat oil in large saucepan over medium heat. Add onion and sauté until translucent. Add tomato paste, lemon juice, sugar, raisins, prunes and apricots. Stir in water and heat to a simmer. Form turkey into small balls (recipe makes about 24 meatballs). Add meatballs to pan, cover and simmer for 1/2 hour, or until cooked through.

Serves 4.

turkey mixed bean chili

Nutrition notes:
Beans are excellent sources of protein and fibre, but canned beans can be high in sodium. Put canned beans in a sieve and rinse them with cold water to reduce the sodium content.

Nutritional analysis per serving:
399 calories
34 g protein
5 g fat
1 g saturated fat
53 g carbohydrate
63 mg cholesterol
1005 mg sodium
12 g fibre

Use any combination of beans you like. Using black beans instead of chickpeas makes a thicker, "beanier" chili.

1 Tbsp	oil	15 mL
1	onion, chopped	1
1 cup	diced celery	240 mL
1	clove garlic, crushed	1
1 lb	ground turkey breast	450 g
1 1/2 cups	green beans, cut into 1-in (2.5-cm) lengths	360 mL
1	12-oz (340-mL) can corn kernels	1
1	28-oz (796-mL) can stewed tomatoes	1
1	14-oz (398-mL) can kidney beans, drained and rinsed	1
1	19-oz (540-mL) can garbanzo beans, drained and rinsed	1
1 Tbsp	chili powder	15 mL
1 tsp	dried oregano	5 mL
1/4 tsp	red pepper flakes	1.2 mL

Heat oil in large pot over medium heat. Add onion, celery and garlic and sauté until vegetables are softened. Add ground turkey and sauté until turkey meat is cooked, about 10 minutes. Add remaining ingredients. Cover and bring to a simmer. Simmer for 10 minutes, or until green beans are just cooked.

Serves 6.

Timesaver tip:
Make this ahead and freeze it. It's a perfect quick meal with crusty bread and a mixed green salad.

turkey meatloaf

Nutrition notes:
Ground turkey breast is much leaner than extra-lean ground beef, but the fat content varies. Make sure you buy ground turkey that is less than 6% fat and does not have turkey skin in the mixture.

Nutritional analysis per serving:
200 calories
18 g protein
10 g fat
3 g saturated fat
49 g carbohydrate
99 mg cholesterol
355 mg sodium
1 g fibre

Try adding grated zucchini or specialty mushrooms, such as porcini or shiitake, to this hearty meatloaf. Serve with chutney or mustard.

2 tsp	oil	10 mL
1	medium onion, diced	1
2 cups	sliced mushrooms	475 mL
2	green onions, chopped	2
1	carrot, shredded	1
1	clove garlic, minced	1
1^1/$_2$ tsp	basil	7.5 mL
1^1/$_2$ lbs	ground turkey breast	680 g
1	egg	1
^{1}/$_2$ cup	bread crumbs	120 mL
2 Tbsp	Parmesan cheese	30 mL
^{1}/$_2$ tsp	salt	2.5 mL
^{1}/$_2$ tsp	ground black pepper	2.5 mL
	dash hot pepper sauce	
2 Tbsp	ketchup	30 mL

Preheat oven to 350°F (175°C). Heat oil in medium skillet over medium heat. Sauté onion, mushrooms, green onion, carrot, garlic and basil until vegetables are soft.

In bowl, combine turkey, egg, bread crumbs, cooked vegetables, Parmesan, salt, pepper and hot pepper sauce. Mix well. Press turkey mixture into 8- x 4-in (20- x 10-cm) loaf pan lined with foil. Brush with ketchup. Bake for 1 hour and 20 minutes. Let stand for 10 minutes before slicing.

Serves 8.

Timesaver tip:
Freeze leftovers in individual slices for quick turkey burgers. Serve in fresh kaiser buns with Dijon mustard, lettuce and sliced tomatoes.

turkey shepherd's pie

Nutrition notes:
You don't need to add fat for smooth, creamy mashed potatoes—just add plenty of milk or chicken broth.

This is a delicious, lower-fat alternative to the traditional beef shepherd's pie. Mushrooms, zucchini or corn kernels can be added to this dish to boost the fibre content.

Nutritional analysis per serving:
234 calories
16 g protein
6 g fat
2 g saturated fat
28 g carbohydrate
56 mg cholesterol
322 mg sodium
5 g fibre

5	medium potatoes, peeled and cubed	5
1	medium rutabaga, peeled and cubed	1
$1/4$ cup	skim milk	60 mL
$1/4$ tsp	salt	1.2 mL
	ground black pepper to taste	
$1^1/4$ lbs	ground turkey breast	565 g
1	medium onion, diced	1
1	clove garlic, minced	1
$3/4$ lb	carrots, diced	340 g
$1/2$ lb	fresh green beans, steamed and cut into bite-sized pieces	225 g
1 tsp	dried thyme	5 mL
$3/4$ cup	chicken broth	180 mL
1 Tbsp	flour	15 mL

Preheat oven to 350°F (175°C). Cook potatoes and rutabaga in boiling water until soft. Drain. Add milk. Beat with mixer or mash until very smooth. Add salt and pepper. Set aside.

Sauté ground turkey in non-stick pan over medium heat until cooked through. Add onion and sauté until translucent. Add garlic, carrots and beans and cook for about 3 minutes. Add thyme and chicken broth. Sprinkle flour over top and cook until thickened. Transfer mixture to 9- x 13-in (23- x 33-cm) baking pan. Spread potato-rutabaga mixture evenly over top. Bake, uncovered, for 30 minutes, or until top is slightly golden.

Serves 8.

lemon dill salmon in parchment paper

Nutrition notes:
Different types of salmon have different amounts of omega-3 fatty acids. Spring salmon, with its higher overall fat content, has the highest amount of omega-3 fats. But pink salmon has only $^1/_3$ the fat of spring salmon, yet $^2/_3$ the amount of omega-3 fatty acids.

Nutritional analysis per serving:
216 calories
26 g protein
10 g fat
2 g saturated fat
5 g carbohydrate
51 mg cholesterol
200 mg sodium
2 g fibre

This looks so elegant, but is simple to prepare. Fish cooked in parchment paper is moister and retains all the flavour of the vegetables.

1 lb	salmon fillet, cut into 4 pieces	450 g
1	red bell pepper, cut into thin strips	1
1	small zucchini, cut into thin 2-in (5-cm) strips	1
2 Tbsp	chopped fresh dill	30 mL
1 Tbsp	olive oil	15 mL
	juice of 1 lemon	
$^1/_4$ tsp	salt	1.2 mL
	ground black pepper to taste	

Preheat oven to 450°F (230°C). Lay out 4 pieces of parchment paper cut into 12-in (30-cm) lengths. Place one salmon piece in middle of each piece of parchment. Arrange red pepper and zucchini beside salmon pieces. Sprinkle chopped dill on salmon. Sprinkle olive oil, lemon juice, salt and pepper over salmon and vegetables. Fold parchment paper over top of package and tuck ends underneath to keep juices inside package.

Place packages in one layer on shallow baking sheet. Bake for 15–20 minutes, or until fish is done. (Allow 10 minutes per inch/2.5 cm of thickness, measured at thickest point.) Serve in parchment paper.

Serves 4.

Timesaver tip:
Make these packets early and put them on a baking sheet in the fridge. Pop in the oven 15–20 minutes before serving time.

bbq salmon in soy sauce marinade

Nutritional analysis per serving:
219 calories
25 g protein
11 g fat
2 g saturated fat
5 g carbohydrate
71 mg cholesterol
568 mg sodium
0 g fibre

This marinade can be used with any fish, but it's especially delicious with salmon. Grill vegetables along with the fish for a quick side dish.

1 lb	salmon fillet	450 g
1/4 cup	soy sauce	60 mL
1/3 cup	vinegar	80 mL
1/4 cup	water	60 mL
1 Tbsp	olive oil	15 mL
1 1/2 Tbsp	honey	22.5 mL
1/4 cup	finely diced onion	60 mL

Place salmon skin side up in glass baking pan. In small bowl, combine soy sauce, vinegar, water, oil, honey and onion. Pour marinade over fish. Marinate in the fridge for 1/2–1 hour. Baste fish frequently.

Barbecue fish for 10 minutes per inch/2.5 cm, flipping fish over halfway through cooking.

Serves 4.

Timesaver tip:
Brush salmon fillet with teriyaki sauce and grated ginger before cooking. Barbecue as above.

salmon and artichoke hearts in phyllo pastry

Nutrition notes:
Phyllo pastry has less than 1 gram of fat per sheet—it's the butter or other fats usually spread between the layers that makes phyllo pastry rich. You can reduce the fat in most phyllo recipes and still have a tasty dish.

Nutritional analysis per serving:
294 calories
27 g protein
12 g fat
2 g saturated fat
15 g carbohydrate
71 mg cholesterol
426 mg sodium
1 g fibre

Phyllo pastry transforms an ordinary meal into an elegant one. Serve with wild rice and roasted asparagus spears for a simple, but special meal.

1 tsp	oil	5 mL
1 cup	sliced mushrooms	240 mL
1	14-oz (398-mL) can artichoke hearts, drained	1
1/4 tsp	salt	1.2 mL
1/8 tsp	ground black pepper	.5 mL
1/4 cup	white wine	60 mL
	rind of 1 small lemon, grated	
4	sheets phyllo pastry	4
1 lb	salmon fillet	450 g
	oil spray	

Preheat oven to 375°F (190°C). Heat oil in non-stick frying pan over medium heat. Add mushrooms and sauté until lightly browned. Cut artichoke hearts into quarters and add to mushrooms. Sauté for 1 more minute. Add salt, pepper, wine and lemon rind. Continue to sauté until all liquid has evaporated. Set aside.

Place one sheet phyllo pastry on large cutting board. Spray lightly with oil. Place another sheet on top and spray with oil. Repeat with all 4 sheets. Place salmon fillet on top of phyllo sheets. Spread artichoke mixture evenly on top of fillet. Wrap salmon and artichoke mixture in pastry, tucking ends under. Place in baking pan and bake for about 30 minutes, or until salmon is done and phyllo pastry is lightly browned. (Allow 10 minutes for each inch/2.5 cm of salmon, measured at thickest point.)

Serves 4.

halibut with mango and red pepper salsa

Nutrition notes:
Combining mangoes and fish provides omega-3 fats from the fish and beta-carotene and vitamin C from the mango—all in one entrée.

Nutritional analysis per serving:
231 calories
25 g protein
6 g fat
1 g saturated fat
18 g carbohydrate
36 mg cholesterol
209 mg sodium
2 g fibre

Nothing beats the flavour of fresh halibut in season. If halibut is not available, this refreshing salsa goes well with poached salmon or baked chicken.

1	mango, peeled and diced	1
1	red bell pepper, diced	1
1/4 cup	chopped white onion	60 mL
1 Tbsp	fresh cilantro	15 mL
	juice of 1 lime	
1 lb	halibut fillets	450 g
1/4 cup	flour	60 mL
1/4 tsp	salt	1.2 mL
1 Tbsp	canola oil	15 mL

Combine mango, red pepper, onion, cilantro and lime juice. Allow mixture to sit for at least 1/2 hour to allow flavours to mingle.

Cut halibut into 4 pieces. Combine flour and salt in plastic bag. Add halibut pieces one at a time and shake bag to coat fish with flour. Heat oil over medium heat in non-stick frying pan. Add halibut and fry until fish is cooked and lightly browned on both sides, about 6 minutes on each side. The fish should be opaque and flake easily when pierced with a fork. Serve halibut topped with plenty of salsa.

Serves 4.

Timesaver tip:
Make the salsa the night before—the flavour will be even better. For a really quick meal, spread a commercial salsa on the fillet and bake.

red snapper in soy ginger sauce

Nutrition notes:
Red snapper, cod, sole and other white fish tend to be lower in omega-3 fatty acids than higher-fat counterparts, such as salmon and trout. However, they are also lower in calories and saturated fat, and can be helpful in maintaining health.

Nutritional analysis per serving:
142 calories
24 g protein
3 g fat
0 g saturated fat
2 g carbohydrate
42 mg cholesterol
846 mg sodium
0 g fibre

Red snapper is a mild-tasting fish with a firm texture. This dish can be considered a "fast food"—it takes only minutes to prepare and cook.

1 lb	red snapper fillets	450 g
1 Tbsp	grated fresh ginger	15 mL
3 Tbsp	soy sauce	45 mL
1/4 cup	white wine	60 mL
1 tsp	oil	5 mL
1 Tbsp	chopped green onions	15 mL

Preheat oven to 400°F (200°C). Place fish in shallow baking dish. Combine all remaining ingredients and pour evenly over fish. Bake uncovered for 15 minutes, or until fish flakes easily with a fork.

Serves 4.

Timesaver tip:
Mix a little teriyaki or soy sauce with grated ginger and pour over fish. Bake as above for a really quick entrée.

curried seafood

Nutrition notes:
Imitation crab, made of white fish such as pollock, is an inexpensive way to enjoy the flavour of crab and reap the benefits of eating fish. Real crab is also low in fat and cholesterol, and can be a delicious part of a heart-healthy diet.

Nutritional analysis per serving:
190 calories
21 g protein
3 g fat
0 g saturated fat
21 g carbohydrate
31 mg cholesterol
1048 mg sodium
3 g fibre

Serve this over rice or noodles. For an elegant luncheon, use real crabmeat and present each serving in a peeled papaya half. Use halibut cut into small chunks instead of scallops, if you prefer.

1 cup	water	240 mL
1/2 lb	fresh scallops	225 g
1 tsp	oil	5 mL
1 cup	chopped onion	240 mL
1	10-oz (284-mL) can mushroom stems and pieces, drained	1
1/2 tsp	garlic powder	2.5 mL
1 tsp	curry powder	5 mL
2 Tbsp	flour	30 mL
1 cup	skim milk	240 mL
1/4 tsp	salt	1.2 mL
1/4 tsp	ground black pepper	1.2 mL
1/2 tsp	sugar	2.5 mL
1/2 lb	imitation crabmeat, shredded	225 g

Bring water to a simmer in medium saucepan. Add scallops and simmer uncovered until cooked, about 3 minutes. Drain and set aside.

Heat oil in medium saucepan over medium heat. Add onion and sauté until softened. Add mushrooms and heat for 1 minute. Add garlic and curry. Stir until mixed. Add flour. Stir and cook over low heat for 1 minute. Add milk slowly, mixing well. Turn heat to medium and bring to a boil, cooking and stirring constantly until thickened. Add salt, pepper and sugar, mixing well. Gently add imitation crab and scallops. Cook until heated through.

Serves 4.

scallop, red pepper and asparagus stir-fry

Nutrition notes:
Sea scallops are about 1¹/₂ in (4 cm) in diameter. Bay scallops tend to be much smaller. Bivalves, such as clams, scallops, oysters and mussels, are excellent protein sources and are low in saturated fat and cholesterol.

Nutritional analysis per serving:
263 calories
33 g protein
10 g fat
1 g saturated fat
11 g carbohydrate
60 mg cholesterol
900 mg sodium
3 g fibre

Scallops are expensive, but cutting them in slices stretches out the amount. Substitute sliced chicken breast or tofu cubes for the scallops, if you like. Serve this over rice or rice noodles.

¹/₂ lb	sea scallops	225 g
3 Tbsp	water	45 mL
1 tsp	cornstarch	5 mL
1 tsp	oyster sauce	5 mL
1 Tbsp	soy sauce	15 mL
1 Tbsp	oil	15 mL
1 lb	asparagus, cut into 1¹/₂-in (4-cm) pieces on the diagonal	450 g
1	red bell pepper, sliced into bite-sized strips	1
1 Tbsp	peeled and minced fresh ginger ground black pepper to taste	15 mL

Slice each scallop into three rounds. Set aside. Combine water, cornstarch, oyster sauce and soy sauce. Set aside.

Heat oil in wok over medium heat and sauté asparagus and red pepper until tender-crisp. Add ginger and scallops. Cook until scallops become white and opaque. Whisk soy sauce mixture with pepper, add to pan and cook until sauce thickens.

Serves 2.

steamed clams

Nutrition notes:
The seasoned broth used for steaming is very flavourful—delicious for dipping instead of melted butter.

Nutritional analysis per serving:
187 calories
13 g protein
4 g fat
0 g saturated fat
13 g carbohydrate
29 mg cholesterol
66 mg sodium
2 g fibre

When you pick your own clams at the market, make sure none of the shells are cracked. Serve the clams and broth in pasta-style bowls and provide fresh crusty bread for soaking up the broth. A crisp green salad completes the meal.

1 tsp	olive oil	5 mL
1/2	onion, chopped	1/2
2	cloves garlic, chopped	2
1	tomato, chopped	1
3/4 cup	white wine	180 mL
1 1/2 lbs	clams	680 g

Heat oil in medium saucepan over medium heat. Add onion and sauté until translucent. Reduce heat. Add garlic and cook 1 minute. Add tomato and cook 1 minute.

Turn heat to high. Add wine and clams. Cover and steam until shells open, about 5 minutes.

Serves 2.

vegetarian chili

Nutrition notes:
Soups, stews and chilies are simple solutions to making healthy, one-pot meals. Protein, starch and vegetables can be combined in an infinite number of ways to provide interesting, nutritious meals.

Nutritional analysis per serving:
213 calories
10 g protein
3 g fat
0 g saturated fat
40 g carbohydrate
0 mg cholesterol
744 mg sodium
11 g fibre

Maple baked beans in tomato sauce is an unusual ingredient for a chili, but it rounds out the acidity of the tomatoes to give the dish a smooth taste. This chili can become a tasty stew just by leaving out the chili powder.

1 Tbsp	oil	15 mL
1	onion, chopped	1
1	clove garlic, minced	1
1	stalk celery, diced	1
3	carrots, peeled and sliced	3
2 cups	zucchini, sliced	475 mL
1/2 cup	water	120 mL
1	19-oz (540-mL) can kidney beans, drained	1
1	14-oz (398-mL) can stewed tomatoes	1
1	14-oz (398-mL) can maple baked beans in tomato sauce	1
2 tsp	chili powder	10 mL

Heat oil in large pot over medium heat. Add onion and garlic and sauté until onions are soft. Add remaining ingredients and bring to a boil. Cover and simmer, stirring often, for 15 minutes. Uncover pot. Simmer, stirring often, for 15 more minutes.

Serves 6.

bulgur bean chili

Nutrition notes:
Bulgur is a form of wheat that has been steamed, dried and crushed. It adds a chewy texture and plenty of fibre and iron to a recipe. Use bulgur in tabbouleh salad, wheat pilaf or vegetarian casseroles.

Nutritional analysis per serving:
295 calories
12 g protein
4 g fat
0 g saturated fat
53 g carbohydrate
0 mg cholesterol
811 mg sodium
14 g fibre

Top each bowl of chili with diced tomatoes, chopped purple onions and a dollop of yogurt before serving.

1 Tbsp	oil	15 mL
1	onion, chopped	1
2	cloves garlic, minced	2
3	carrots, chopped	3
1 cup	sliced mushrooms	240 mL
1	small jalapeño pepper, minced	1
1	red bell pepper, diced	1
1 Tbsp	chili powder	15 mL
1 tsp	ground cumin	5 mL
1	28-oz (796-mL) can plum tomatoes	1
1 tsp	brown sugar	5 mL
3/4 cup	water	180 mL
1	14-oz (398-mL) can kidney beans, rinsed	1
1	19-oz (540-mL) can chickpeas, rinsed	1
1/2 cup	bulgur	120 mL

Heat oil in large saucepan over medium heat. Add onion and sauté for 2 minutes. Add garlic, carrots, mushrooms, jalapeño pepper, red pepper, chili powder and cumin. Sauté until vegetables are soft, about 5 minutes. Add tomatoes, sugar and water. Bring to a boil and cook for 5 minutes. Reduce heat to low. Add beans and chickpeas, cover and cook for 1/2 hour.

Add bulgur and cook uncovered for 15 minutes, or until bulgur is soft. Add more water if chili becomes too thick.

Serves 6.

chickpea stew

Nutrition notes:
Have a vegetarian meal
with beans, lentils or tofu
at least once per week.
Your diet will be lower in
saturated fat and higher
in fibre, phytochemicals,
phytoestrogens and other
nutrients that promote
good health.

**Nutritional analysis
per serving:**
290 calories
10 g protein
7 g fat
1 g saturated fat
47 g carbohydrate
0 mg cholesterol
1105 mg sodium
10 g fibre

This is a great source of fibre, especially if served over brown rice. Add diced zucchini or sliced mushrooms to boost the vegetable content.

2 Tbsp	olive oil	30 mL
$1/4$ tsp	ground black pepper	1.2 mL
1	medium onion, sliced	1
1 Tbsp	ground cumin	15 mL
$1/2$ tsp	curry powder	2.5 mL
1	14-oz (398-mL) can tomatoes, crushed	1
2	19-oz (540-mL) cans chickpeas, drained and rinsed	2
1	medium eggplant, cubed	1
$1^1/2$ tsp	soy sauce	7.5 mL

Heat oil in medium pot over medium heat. Stir in black pepper. Add onion and sauté until golden. Add cumin and curry powder. Continue cooking until spices become aromatic, about 2 minutes. Add tomatoes and cook for 5 minutes.

Add chickpeas and eggplant. Cover and simmer over low heat for 30 minutes. Remove cover and cook for 15 minutes longer to allow some of the moisture to evaporate. Stir in soy sauce.

Serves 6.

sautéed vegetable pizza

Nutrition notes:
Restaurant pizza is laden with cheese and high-fat meats. Make your own pizza with chopped chicken bits or shredded lean ham, lots of vegetables and just a sprinkle of low-fat cheese. This makes a scrumptious meal with plenty of nutrition.

Nutritional analysis per serving:
299 calories
14 g protein
7 g fat
2 g saturated fat
47 g carbohydrate
10 mg cholesterol
501 mg sodium
9 g fibre

Make this pizza when you have many leftover bits of vegetables. Any vegetables will work, but the caramelized onions definitely boost the flavour.

1 tsp	oil	5 mL
1	onion, sliced	1
1 cup	mushrooms, sliced	240 mL
2 cups	cauliflower florets	475 mL
2 cups	broccoli florets	475 mL
1	red bell pepper, sliced	1
	salt and ground black pepper to taste	
1	12-in (30-cm) precooked pizza crust	1
3	Roma tomatoes, diced	3
1/2 cup	grated low-fat mozzarella cheese	120 mL

Preheat oven to 375°F (190°C). Heat oil in large non-stick frying pan over medium heat. Add onion and sauté until slightly browned. Add mushrooms and sauté until slightly cooked, about 2 minutes. Add cauliflower, broccoli and red pepper and sauté until broccoli is bright green and tender-crisp, about 5 minutes. Season with salt and pepper.

Remove from heat. Place pizza crust on large baking sheet. Spread sautéed vegetables over pizza crust. Sprinkle with fresh tomatoes. Sprinkle grated cheese over pizza. Bake until cheese is melted and crust is hot.

Serves 4.

Timesaver tip:
If you have leftover roasted or barbecued vegetables, just spread them over the pizza crust, top with fresh tomatoes, sprinkle with grated low-fat cheese and bake.

soybean brown rice casserole

Nutrition notes:
It is easy on busy days to forgo making vegetables, and to eat just a casserole alone. Despite how healthy a casserole might be, eating multiple portions can add more calories than you may want. Be sure to include vegetables, in addition to your casserole, to help add bulk as well as nutrition to your meal.

Nutritional analysis per serving:
374 calories
17 g protein
10 g fat
1 g saturated fat
58 g carbohydrate
0 mg cholesterol
367 mg sodium
8 g fibre

Soybeans, brown rice and corn are a nutritious combination. They give an interesting texture to this tasty casserole.

1 cup	dried soybeans	240 mL
1 Tbsp	oil	15 mL
1	onion, chopped	1
2	stalks celery, chopped	2
4 cups	cooked brown rice	950 mL
1	15-oz (425-mL) can herb-flavoured stewed tomatoes	1
2 cups	corn kernels	475 mL
1/2 tsp	salt	2.5 mL
1/4 tsp	ground black pepper	1.2 mL
1/2 tsp	dried thyme	2.5 mL

Soak soybeans in 4 cups (950 mL) water for 8 hours or overnight. Drain. Cook beans in 6 cups (1.5 L) water for 1½–2 hours, or until tender. Drain.

Preheat oven to 350°F (175°C). Heat oil in frying pan over medium heat. Add onion and celery and sauté until soft. Combine cooked soybeans, sautéed onions and celery, rice, tomatoes, corn, salt, pepper and thyme in 2-qt (2-L) casserole dish with cover. Cover and bake for 40 minutes, or until casserole is hot.

Serves 6.

Timesaver tip:
Use 1 can of garbanzo beans instead of making soybeans from scratch. Cook casserole in microwave until hot.

soy macaroni casserole

Nutrition notes:
Soy-based imitation ground meats have the texture of ground meat, but the benefits of soy. If you prefer the flavour of meat, replace half the soy products with ground meat.

Nutritional analysis per serving:
546 calories
22 g protein
11 g fat
2 g saturated fat
88 g carbohydrate
5 mg cholesterol
864 mg sodium
9 g fibre

A super-easy dish that's rather homey. Vegetarian ground round is a soy-based meat substitute that can usually be found next to the tofu and other soy products at the supermarket.

1 Tbsp	oil	15 mL
1	onion, chopped	1
2 cups	sliced mushrooms	475 mL
1	12-oz (340-g) pkg vegetarian ground round	1
1	10-oz (284-mL) can tomato soup	1
1 cup	water	240 mL
5 cups	cooked macaroni	1.2 L
1	12-oz (340-mL) can corn kernels	1
$^1/_4$ cup	grated light Cheddar cheese	60 mL

Preheat oven to 350°F (175°C). Heat oil in sauté pan over medium heat. Add onion and mushrooms and sauté until lightly browned. Add vegetarian ground round and cook until slightly browned. Add tomato soup, water, cooked macaroni and corn. Stir until combined.

Pour into 2-qt (2-L) casserole dish with cover. Sprinkle with cheese. Cover and bake for 30 minutes.

Serves 4.

pasta primavera with tofu

Nutrition notes:
Tofu comes in a variety of firmness—the firmer it is, the higher the protein, unsaturated fat and phytochemical content. Soy products such as tofu are especially high in phytoestrogens. All types of tofu contain beneficial nutrients, so choose the firmness that best suits your recipe and preference.

Nutritional analysis per serving:
590 calories
30 g protein
13 g fat
2 g saturated fat
90 g carbohydrate
0 mg cholesterol
976 mg sodium
9 g fibre

For newcomers to tofu, this recipe is a good place to begin! Tofu is bland on its own, but takes on the flavour of the seasonings it's cooked with. The firm herbed tofu adds interesting texture to the sauce.

1 Tbsp	olive oil	15 mL
2 cups	finely chopped onion	475 mL
3	cloves garlic, diced	3
1 cup	finely chopped carrots	240 mL
1	12-oz (340-g) pkg firm herbed tofu, drained and crumbled	1
1 cup	grated zucchini	240 mL
1 cup	sliced mushrooms	240 mL
2 Tbsp	soy sauce	30 mL
2 Tbsp	tomato paste	30 mL
1	28-oz (796-mL) can peeled plum tomatoes, mashed	1
	dash cayenne pepper	
1 tsp	dried basil	5 mL
1 tsp	dried oregano	5 mL
	salt and ground black pepper to taste	
³/₄ lb	dried penne	340 g

Heat oil in medium saucepan over high heat. Add onion, garlic and carrots, reduce heat to medium and sauté until onions are golden. Stir in tofu. Add zucchini, mushrooms, soy sauce and tomato paste.

Timesaver tip:
Make this pasta dish when you have leftover cooked vegetables, such as carrots and zucchini. Place chopped vegetables, crumbled tofu and commercial pasta sauce in a pot. Simmer for 15 minutes, toss with pasta and serve.

Stir until mixed. Add tomatoes, cayenne pepper, basil and oregano and stir thoroughly. Season with salt and pepper. Cover and simmer over low heat for 1 hour, stirring occasionally.

Cook pasta according to package directions. Toss with sauce just before serving.

Serves 4.

vegetarian mexican lasagna

Nutrition notes:
Tortillas, traditionally baked on a griddle, contain minimal fat and are made from wheat or corn flour. They are a nice change from bread and can be used for wraps, burritos, fajitas or even chips.

Nutritional analysis per serving:
336 calories
31 g protein
8 g fat
2 g saturated fat
37 g carbohydrate
64 mg cholesterol
840 mg sodium
5 g fibre

This is a tasty twist on traditional lasagna—it uses corn tortillas instead of noodles and soy-based ground round instead of ground beef. You will find it truly difficult to believe this delicious dish contains no meat.

1 Tbsp	oil	15 mL
1	onion, chopped	1
1	clove garlic, crushed	1
1	12-oz (340-g) pkg vegetarian ground round	1
1/2 cup	salsa	120 mL
1/2 tsp	ground cumin	2.5 mL
1 Tbsp	chili powder	15 mL
1/2 tsp	ground black pepper	2.5 mL
1 Tbsp	Louisiana hot sauce	15 mL
1	14-oz (398-mL) can stewed tomatoes	1
	juice of 1 lime	
2 cups	1% cottage cheese	475 mL
1	egg, beaten	1
1/2 tsp	ground cumin	2.5 mL
1 tsp	Louisiana hot sauce	5 mL
10	6-in (15-cm) corn tortillas	10
1/2 cup	grated light Cheddar cheese	120 mL

Preheat oven to 350°F (175°C). Heat oil in medium non-stick frying pan over medium heat. Add onion and garlic and sauté until onions are softened. Add vegetarian ground round (breaking into small bits), salsa, 1/2 tsp (2.5 mL) cumin, chili powder, pepper, 1 Tbsp (15 mL) hot sauce, stewed tomatoes and lime juice. Continue to simmer for about 10 minutes. Remove from heat.

In medium bowl, combine cottage cheese, egg, remaining 1/2 tsp (2.5 mL) cumin and 1 tsp (5 mL) hot sauce. Set aside.

To assemble lasagna, layer ½ of tortillas on bottom of 9- x 13-in (23- x 33-cm) pan, breaking tortillas in half to cover bottom of pan. Spread half of the tomato mixture onto tortillas, followed by all of the cottage cheese mixture. Top with remaining tomato mixture. Cover with remaining tortillas. Sprinkle with grated cheese.

Bake covered for 25 minutes. Uncover and bake for additional 10 minutes. Let sit for 10 minutes before serving.

Serves 8.

Timesaver tip:
Using vegetarian ground round instead of ground beef saves time in that it is precooked. Sauté onions with vegetarian ground round, add bottled spaghetti sauce and serve over pasta for a quick, satisfying meal.

polenta with sautéed vegetables

Nutrition notes:
Healthy eating can be entertaining and exciting, especially when you take advantage of the cuisine of many cultures. Sushi, polenta, pizza, stir-fries and hummus are just a few examples of healthy international cuisine.

Nutritional analysis per serving:
287 calories
9 g protein
7 g fat
2 g saturated fat
50 g carbohydrate
5 mg cholesterol
633 g sodium
7 g fibre

You can also make individual servings by slicing the cooled polenta into 4 pieces. Top each serving with the vegetable mixture and cheese, and bake.

$^1/_2$ tsp	salt	2.5 mL
$3^1/_2$ cups	water	840 mL
$1^1/_4$ cups	cornmeal	300 mL
1 tsp	dried oregano	5 mL
1 Tbsp	grated light Parmesan cheese	15 mL
1 Tbsp	oil	15 mL
2	cloves garlic, minced	2
$^1/_2$	red onion, chopped	$^1/_2$
$1^1/_2$ cups	sliced mushrooms	360 mL
2 cups	sliced zucchini	475 mL
1	red bell pepper, sliced	1
1	14-oz (398-mL) can stewed tomatoes	1
2 Tbsp	chopped fresh basil	30 mL
$^1/_4$ tsp	ground black pepper	1.2 mL
$^1/_4$ cup	grated light Parmesan cheese	60 mL

Bring salt and water to a boil in medium pot. Reduce heat to medium-low. Add cornmeal very gradually, stirring constantly to prevent lumping. Cook and stir until cornmeal is very thick, about 10 minutes.

Mix in oregano and 1 Tbsp (15 mL) Parmesan cheese. Spread evenly into greased 9- x 13-in (23- x 33-cm) baking dish. Let cool.

Preheat oven to 400°F (200°C). Heat oil in frying pan over medium-high heat. Add garlic, onion and mushrooms and sauté until slightly browned.

Add zucchini and red pepper and sauté until just tender. Add stewed tomatoes, basil and black pepper. Cook 1 more minute. Spread vegetable mixture on top of cooled polenta. Sprinkle with $1/4$ cup (60 mL) Parmesan cheese. Bake for 15 minutes, or until polenta is hot and cheese is melted. Cut into 4 pieces.

Serves 4.

Timesaver tip:
Cut the polenta into serving sizes, top with your favourite pasta sauce and heat in the microwave. Serve with a simple salad.

vegetable curry

Nutrition notes:
Using vegetables of different colour in a dish will ensure that a variety of flavonoids are a part of your meal.

Nutritional analysis per serving:
211 calories
7 g protein
3 g fat
0 g saturated fat
41 g carbohydrate
0 mg cholesterol
605 mg sodium
9 g fibre

Any vegetable mixture is good in this flavourful curry. It is especially tasty over brown rice.

1 Tbsp	oil	15 mL
1 cup	chopped onion	240 mL
1 cup	chopped celery	240 mL
1 Tbsp	curry powder	15 mL
1 Tbsp	turmeric	15 mL
$1/2$ tsp	red pepper flakes	2.5 mL
$1^1/2$ cups	hot water	360 mL
1	vegetable bouillon cube	1
1	28-oz (796-mL) can stewed tomatoes	1
2	medium parsnips, sliced	2
3	medium carrots, sliced	3
3	potatoes, peeled and cut into 1-in (2.5-cm) cubes	3
2 cups	cauliflower florets	475 mL
2 cups	green beans, cut into 1-in (2.5-cm) lengths	475 mL
2	19-oz (540-mL) cans chickpeas, drained	2
$1/2$ cup	chopped dried apricots	120 mL

Heat oil in large soup pot over medium heat. Add onion, celery, curry powder, turmeric and pepper flakes. Sauté until onion and celery are softened.

Combine hot water and bouillon cube and stir until the cube dissolves. Add a little to onion mixture as necessary to prevent burning. When onion and celery are soft, add remainder of broth, tomatoes, parsnips, carrots, potatoes and cauliflower to pot. Cook for 15 minutes. Add green beans, chickpeas and dried apricots, and cook for another 10 minutes, or until all vegetables are soft.

Serves 12.

baked goods

lemon poppy-seed loaf

Nutrition notes:
Although eggs are nutritious, the yolks are very high in dietary cholesterol. To reduce the cholesterol in baked goods, substitute 2 egg whites for 1 whole egg.

Nutritional analysis per slice:
161 calories
3 g protein
5 g fat
0 g saturated fat
27 g carbohydrate
16 mg cholesterol
75 mg sodium
1 g fibre

This loaf is like a light pound cake with a lemon tang. Poppy seeds add crunch and nutty flavour.

1 cup	granulated sugar	240 mL
1/4 cup	canola oil	60 mL
1	egg	1
2	egg whites	2
1 Tbsp	lemon rind	15 mL
1 tsp	lemon juice	5 mL
2 Tbsp	poppy seeds	30 mL
1 tsp	vanilla extract	5 mL
1²/₃ cups	flour	400 mL
1 tsp	baking powder	5 mL
1/4 tsp	baking soda	1.2 mL
3/4 cup	low-fat buttermilk	180 mL
1/4 cup	icing sugar	60 mL
2 Tbsp	lemon juice	30 mL

Preheat oven to 350°F (175°). Line 8- x 4-in (20- x 10-cm) loaf pan with foil, or spray with non-stick spray.

In large bowl, beat granulated sugar and oil until creamy. Add egg and egg whites, one at a time, beating well after each addition. Beat in lemon rind, 1 tsp (5 mL) lemon juice, poppy seeds and vanilla. Set aside.

In separate bowl, mix together flour, baking powder and soda. Add dry ingredients alternately with buttermilk to sugar mixture. Mix well. Pour into prepared loaf pan. Bake for 1 hour, or until toothpick inserted into centre comes out clean. Let cool for 10 minutes.

Mix together icing sugar and 2 Tbsp (30 mL) lemon juice. Poke holes in top of loaf, using a toothpick. Brush glaze over loaf.

Makes 15 slices.

harvest pumpkin loaf

Nutrition notes:
Pumpkin is a good source of beta-carotene. Make homemade pumpkin purée in the fall when fresh pumpkins are plentiful. Cut pumpkin into chunks and bake at 350°F (175°C) until soft. Remove skin and purée pumpkin until smooth. Drain off any excess liquid. Freeze in small containers.

Nutritional analysis per slice:
138 calories
3 g protein
5 g fat
1 g saturated fat
22 g carbohydrate
32 mg cholesterol
185 mg sodium
1 g fibre

This is also delicious with dried cranberries in place of the raisins.

1 cup	canned pumpkin purée	240 mL
1/4 cup	canola oil	60 mL
2	eggs, beaten	2
1/4 tsp	nutmeg	1.2 mL
1/4 tsp	ground cinnamon	1.2 mL
1 Tbsp	molasses	15 mL
1 1/2 cups	flour	360 mL
1/2 tsp	salt	2.5 mL
1 tsp	baking soda	5 mL
1/2 cup	sugar	120 mL
1/2 cup	raisins	120 mL

Preheat oven to 350°F (175°C). Spray 8- x 4-in (20- x 10-cm) loaf pan with non-stick spray, or line with foil.

In medium bowl, combine pumpkin, oil, eggs, nutmeg, cinnamon and molasses. Beat well.

In separate bowl, mix together flour, salt, baking soda and sugar. Add dry ingredients to batter and combine until thoroughly mixed. Stir in raisins. Pour batter into prepared loaf pan. Bake for 1 hour, or until toothpick inserted in centre comes out clean. Cool on rack before slicing.

Makes 15 slices.

apple cinnamon loaf

Nutrition notes:
Not only are apples high in pectin, a soluble fibre, they are also loaded with flavonoids—all the more reason for eating an apple a day!

Nutritional analysis per slice:
157 calories
3 g protein
4 g fat
0 g saturated fat
28 g carbohydrate
1 mg cholesterol
175 mg sodium
2 g fibre

MacIntosh apples are juicy and flavourful, but you can use any apples. Try raisins or coarsely chopped dried apricots instead of cranberries.

1 cup	all-purpose flour	240 mL
$3/4$ cup	whole-wheat flour	180 mL
$1^1/2$ tsp	ground cinnamon	7.5 mL
$1/2$ tsp	nutmeg	2.5 mL
1 tsp	baking soda	5 mL
1 tsp	baking powder	5 mL
$1/4$ tsp	salt	1.2 mL
$1/4$ cup	canola oil	60 mL
$1/2$ cup	brown sugar, packed	120 mL
$1/4$ cup	egg whites (or 2 egg whites)	60 mL
$3/4$ cup	low-fat vanilla yogurt	180 mL
$1^1/4$ cups	peeled, grated apple	300 mL
$3/4$ cup	dried cranberries	180 mL

Preheat oven to 350°F (175°C). Spray 8- x 4-in (20- x 10-cm) loaf pan with non-stick spray, or line with foil.

Combine flours, cinnamon, nutmeg, baking soda, baking powder and salt in bowl. Set aside.

In separate large bowl, combine oil and brown sugar. Mix well. Beat in egg whites. Add yogurt and beat well. Stir in apple and cranberries. Add flour mixture. Stir until just combined. Pour into prepared loaf pan. Bake for 50 minutes, or until toothpick inserted in centre of loaf comes out clean. Cool on rack before cutting.

Makes 15 slices.

Timesaver tip:
Wrap each slice individually in plastic wrap and freeze for a lunch bag treat.

zucchini carrot loaf

Nutrition notes:
Zucchini bread and carrot cakes are usually high in oil or other fats. Using yogurt or buttermilk provides moisture with much less fat.

Nutritional analysis per slice:
144 calories
3 g protein
4 g fat
0 g saturated fat
24 g carbohydrate
16 mg cholesterol
146 mg sodium
1 g fibre

There are more vegetables than fruit in this healthy, tasty loaf. If you prefer, substitute dried cranberries or cherries for the raisins.

1	egg	1
2	egg whites	2
1/4 cup	canola oil	60 mL
1/4 cup	plain low-fat yogurt	60 mL
3/4 cup	sugar	180 mL
1 tsp	vanilla extract	5 mL
1 1/2 cups	flour	360 mL
1 tsp	baking soda	5 mL
1 tsp	ground cinnamon	5 mL
1/4 tsp	salt	1.2 mL
1/2 cup	grated carrot	120 mL
1/2 cup	grated zucchini	120 mL
1/2 cup	raisins	120 mL

Preheat oven to 350°F (175°C). Line 8- x 4-in (20- x 10-cm) loaf pan with foil, or spray with non-stick spray.

In medium bowl, mix together egg, egg whites, oil, yogurt, sugar and vanilla. Beat until blended. In separate bowl, mix together flour, baking soda, cinnamon and salt. Stir into egg mixture. Mix in carrot, zucchini and raisins. Pour into prepared loaf pan. Bake for 1 hour, or until toothpick inserted into centre comes out clean. Cool on rack before slicing.

Makes 15 slices.

maple cornbread

Nutrition notes:
Cornmeal bread, with its rather crunchy texture, is a nice change from other sweet breads. Cornmeal is high in fibre and phytosterols.

Nutritional analysis per slice:
76 calories
2 g protein
1 g fat
0 g saturated fat
16 g carbohydrate
8 mg cholesterol
93 mg sodium
1 g fibre

This sweet cornbread is a perfect accompaniment to baked beans. The whole-wheat flour adds a nice nutty flavour and provides extra fibre.

1^3/4 cups	whole-wheat flour	420 mL
1 cup	cornmeal	240 mL
^{1}/2 tsp	salt	2.5 mL
1 tsp	baking soda	5 mL
1	egg, beaten	1
2 cups	buttermilk	475 mL
^{3}/4 cup	maple syrup	180 mL
^{1}/2 cup	raisins	120 mL

Preheat oven to 350°F (175°C). Line two 8- x 4-in (20- x 10-cm) loaf pans with foil, or spray with non-stick spray.

In large bowl, mix together flour, cornmeal, salt and baking soda. In smaller bowl, combine egg, buttermilk and syrup. Stir into flour mixture. Mix well. Stir in raisins.

Pour into prepared pans. Bake for 40 minutes, or until toothpick inserted into centre comes out clean. Cool on rack before slicing.

Makes 2 loaves (30 slices).

Timesaver tip:
This bread freezes nicely, so freeze the extra loaf for another day.

tea bread

Nutritional notes:
Tea contains phenols, which may act as antioxidants in our bodies. Antioxidants have been associated with reduced risk of heart disease.

Nutritional analysis per slice:
141 calories
2 g protein
1 g fat
0 g saturated fat
33 g carbohydrate
14 mg cholesterol
44 mg sodium
1 g fibre

This recipe has absolutely no added fat! It's best if you use a mixture of dried apricots, pears, peaches and prunes. It takes a little more time to make, since the fruit must soak for 1 hour. Try toasting it for breakfast instead of regular bread.

1 cup	cold tea	240 mL
1 cup	brown sugar	240 mL
1 cup	diced dried fruit	240 mL
2 cups	cake flour	475 mL
1 tsp	baking powder	5 mL
1	egg, slightly beaten	1
1 tsp	vanilla extract	5 mL

Preheat oven to 325°F (165°C). Line 8- x 4-in (20- x 10-cm) loaf pan with foil, or spray with non-stick spray.

Combine tea, brown sugar and dried fruit. Let sit for 1 hour.

In medium bowl, combine flour and baking powder. Add egg, vanilla and dried fruit mixture. Mix well. Pour into prepared pan. Bake for 1¼ hours, or until toothpick inserted in centre comes out clean. Cool on rack before slicing.

Makes 15 slices.

Timesaver tip:
If you want to save a little time cutting up the fruit, use a mixture of small fruits—raisins, dried cranberries and cherries.

banana bran muffins

Nutritional analysis per muffin, with chocolate chips:
201 calories
5 g protein
7 g fat
2 g saturated fat
33 g carbohydrate
18 mg cholesterol
250 mg sodium
5 g fibre

Nutritional analysis per muffin, without chocolate chips:
159 calories
5 g protein
5 g fat
1 g saturated fat
28 g carbohydrate
17 mg cholesterol
242 mg sodium
5 g fibre

Each muffin contains 1$^1/_2$ Tbsp (22.5 mL) of bran—a good source of fibre. Chocolate chips are optional, but they make these muffins a real treat.

1$^1/_2$	cupswheat bran	360 mL
1 cup	whole-wheat flour	240 mL
$^1/_2$ cup	all-purpose flour	120 mL
1$^1/_2$ tsp	baking powder	7.5 mL
1 tsp	baking soda	5 mL
$^1/_2$ tsp	salt	2.5 mL
$^1/_2$ cup	dried cranberries	120 mL
$^1/_4$ cup	canola oil	60 mL
$^1/_3$ cup	brown sugar	80 mL
1	egg	1
$^1/_4$ cup	egg whites (or 2 egg whites)	60 mL
3	ripe bananas, mashed	3
1 cup	fat-free yogurt	240 mL
$^1/_2$ cup	chocolate chips (optional)	120 mL

Preheat oven to 375°F (190°C). Spray 15-cup muffin tin with non-stick spray, or line with paper muffin cups.

Combine bran, flours, baking powder, baking soda and salt in bowl. Mix in cranberries. Set aside.

In large bowl, combine oil, brown sugar, egg, egg whites, banana and yogurt. Mix well. Add flour and cranberry mixture. Stir until combined. Add chocolate chips, if desired. Spoon mixture into prepared muffin tin. Bake for 30 minutes, or until toothpick inserted in centre of muffin comes out clean. Serve warm or cooled.

Makes 15 muffins.

rhubarb cranberry muffins

Nutritional analysis per muffin:
207 calories
4 g protein
5 g fat
1 g saturated fat
36 g carbohydrate
18 mg cholesterol
161 mg sodium
1 g fibre

These sweet tangy muffins can be a dessert if baked in a loaf pan.

2 cups	flour	475 mL
$3/4$ cup	sugar	180 mL
1 tsp	baking powder	5 mL
1 tsp	baking soda	5 mL
$1/2$ tsp	salt	2.5 mL
1	egg	1
$1/4$ cup	canola oil	60 mL
1 cup	plain non-fat yogurt	240 mL
1 Tbsp	grated orange rind	15 mL
$1^1/4$ cups	diced rhubarb	300 mL
$1/2$ cup	dried cranberries	120 mL

Preheat oven to 350°F (175°C). Line 12-cup muffin tin with paper muffin cups, or spray with non-stick spray.

In large bowl, mix together flour, sugar, baking powder, baking soda and salt. Set aside.

In separate bowl, beat together egg, oil and yogurt. Mix in orange rind. Add to flour mixture and stir until just combined. Stir in rhubarb and cranberries. Spoon batter into prepared muffin tin. Bake for 25 minutes, or until golden. Serve warm or cooled.

Makes 12 muffins.

Timesaver tip:
Rhubarb stalks can be washed, diced, bagged and frozen for use in most recipes.

banana-carrot-pineapple muffins

Nutrition notes:
Frozen peeled bananas make a delicious low-fat alternative to an ice-cream bar. Peel a banana, wrap it in plastic and freeze. Eat it whole or cut it into pieces.

Nutritional analysis per muffin:
173 calories
3 g protein
6 g fat
1 g saturated fat
29 g carbohydrate
20 mg cholesterol
121 mg sodium
2 g fibre

This is a perfect way to use up overripe bananas.

2^1/$_2$ cups	flour	600 mL
2 tsp	baking soda	10 mL
1 cup	quick rolled oats	240 mL
^{1}/$_2$ cup	canola oil	120 mL
1 cup	sugar	240 mL
2	eggs	2
3	large ripe bananas, mashed	3
1 cup	grated carrot	240 mL
1	14-oz (398-mL) can crushed pineapple, drained	1

Preheat oven to 375°F (190°C). Spray two 12-cup muffin tins with non-stick spray, or line with paper muffin cups.

Combine flour, baking soda and rolled oats in bowl. Set aside. In separate large bowl, combine oil, sugar, eggs, bananas, carrot and pineapple. Add flour mixture to liquid mixture and stir until moistened. Spoon mixture into prepared muffin tins. Bake for 20–25 minutes. Serve warm or cooled.

Makes 24 muffins.

Timesaver tip:
Put overripe bananas in the freezer to use when you have time to bake. Peel bananas when just slightly defrosted for easier handling.

orange muffins

Nutrition notes:
Citrus fruits, such as lemons, oranges and grapefruits, are an excellent source of vitamin C. Add citrus juices to marinades or salad dressings and the zest to baked goods.

Nutritional analysis per muffin:
165 calories
3 g protein
3 g fat
0 g saturated fat
33 g carbohydrate
18 mg cholesterol
246 mg sodium
1 g fibre

Believe it or not, this recipe calls for a whole orange to be puréed!

1	orange	1
1/3 cup	orange juice	80 mL
1	egg	1
3/4 cup	sugar	180 mL
2 Tbsp	canola oil	30 mL
1/4 cup	plain low-fat yogurt	60 mL
1 tsp	vanilla extract	5 mL
1 1/2 cups	flour	360 mL
1 tsp	baking powder	5 mL
1 tsp	baking soda	5 mL
1/4 tsp	salt	1.2 mL
1/2 cup	raisins	120 mL

Preheat oven to 375°F (190°C). Spray 12-cup muffin tin with non-stick spray, or line with paper muffin cups.

Cut orange into 8 wedges. Put orange, orange juice, egg, sugar, oil, yogurt and vanilla into blender or food processor and blend well. If using blender, pour batter into large bowl; otherwise, use food processor bowl.

Combine flour, baking powder, baking soda and salt. Add flour mixture to batter and mix well. Stir in raisins. Spoon mixture into prepared muffin tin. Bake for 20 minutes, or until toothpick inserted into centre of muffin comes out clean. Serve warm or cooled.

Makes 12 muffins.

Timesaver tip:
Buy ready-made low-fat muffin mix. Add raisins or dried cranberries. Prepare according to package directions.

apple bran muffins

Nutrition notes:
Most recipes need a maximum of $1/4$ cup (60 mL) oil or soft margarine per 12 muffins or 1 loaf. Replace the rest of the fat in the recipe with yogurt, applesauce or other puréed fruit.

Nutritional analysis per muffin:
177 calories
4 g protein
6 g fat
1 g saturated fat
30 g carbohydrate
18 mg cholesterol
208 mg sodium
4 g fibre

Apples provide moisture and flavour in these high-fibre muffins.

1 cup	bran	240 mL
1 cup	all-purpose flour	240 mL
$3/4$ cup	whole-wheat flour	180 mL
1 tsp	baking soda	5 mL
1 tsp	baking powder	5 mL
1 tsp	ground cinnamon	5 mL
$1/2$ tsp	nutmeg	2.5 mL
$1/4$ tsp	salt	1.2 mL
1	egg	1
$1/4$ cup	canola oil	60 mL
1 tsp	vanilla extract	5 mL
$1/2$ cup	brown sugar, packed	120 mL
$3/4$ cup	fat-free yogurt	180 mL
$1 1/2$ cups	peeled and shredded apples	360 mL

Preheat oven to 375°F (190°C). Spray 12-cup muffin tin with non-stick spray, or line with paper muffin cups.

Combine bran, all-purpose flour, whole-wheat flour, baking soda, baking powder, cinnamon, nutmeg and salt in mixing bowl.

In separate large bowl, whisk together egg, oil, vanilla, brown sugar and yogurt. Add flour mixture to liquid ingredients and mix until moistened. Add shredded apple and mix until apple is evenly distributed throughout batter. Spoon mixture into prepared muffin tins. Bake for 20 minutes, or until toothpick inserted into centre of muffin comes out clean. Serve warm or cooled.

Makes 12 muffins.

blueberry lemon muffins

Nutrition notes:
Blueberries are rich in antioxidants. Add a handful of fresh or frozen blueberries to baked goods, pancakes, salads or your favourite cereal.

Nutritional analysis per muffin:
201 calories
3 g protein
5 g fat
1 g saturated fat
36 g carbohydrate
20 mg cholesterol
183 mg sodium
1 g fibre

Cranberries or raspberries are just as scrumptious as blueberries in these muffins. If the berries are really sweet, you can use less sugar.

2 cups	flour	475 mL
1^1/$_2$ tsp	baking powder	7.5 mL
^{1}/$_2$ tsp	baking soda	2.5 mL
^{1}/$_4$ tsp	salt	1.2 mL
1 cup	sugar	240 mL
1	egg, beaten	1
^{1}/$_4$ cup	canola oil	60 mL
^{1}/$_4$ cup	lemon juice	60 mL
^{1}/$_2$ cup	skim-milk yogurt	120 mL
2 Tbsp	lemon zest	30 mL
1 cup	frozen or fresh blueberries	240 mL

Preheat oven to 350°F (175°C). Spray 12-cup muffin tin with non-stick spray, or line with paper muffin cups.

Combine flour, baking powder, baking soda and salt in bowl and mix thoroughly.

In separate large bowl, combine sugar, egg, oil, lemon juice, yogurt and lemon zest. Mix well. Add flour mixture to liquid ingredients and mix until moistened. Stir in blueberries. Spoon mixture into prepared muffin tin. Bake for 20 minutes, or until golden. Toothpick inserted into centre of muffin should come out clean. Serve warm or cooled.

Makes 12 muffins.

Timesaver tip:
Make a loaf instead of 1 dozen muffins.

quick drop biscuits

Nutritional analysis per biscuit:
125 calories
3 g protein
5 g fat
0 g saturated fat
18 g carbohydrate
0 mg cholesterol
204 mg sodium
2 g fibre

These biscuits take little time to prepare since they require no rolling or cutting. To vary the recipe, add $^1/_2$ cup (120 mL) blueberries or raisins.

1 cup	all-purpose flour	240 mL
$^3/_4$ cup	whole-wheat flour	180 mL
$^1/_4$ cup	quick oats	60 mL
$^1/_2$ tsp	salt	2.5 mL
2 Tbsp	sugar	30 mL
1 Tbsp	baking powder	15 mL
$^1/_4$ cup	canola oil	60 mL
1 cup	1% buttermilk	240 mL
$^1/_4$ cup	vanilla soy milk	60 mL

Preheat oven to 400°F (200°C). In medium mixing bowl, combine all-purpose flour, whole-wheat flour, oats, salt, sugar and baking powder. Mix well.

In separate small mixing bowl, combine oil, buttermilk and soy milk. Mix well. Add buttermilk mixture to flour mixture. Stir until just mixed. Using large spoon, drop onto non-stick baking sheet. Bake for 12–15 minutes, or until bottoms are golden. Serve warm.

Makes 12 biscuits.

batter beer bread

Nutrition notes:
Although most breads only have a trace of fat, the calories add up quickly. Use spreads such as jam, honey, mustards or low-fat mayonnaise and leave the margarine off.

Nutritional analysis per slice:
167 calories
4 g protein
2 g fat
0 g saturated fat
32 g carbohydrate
0 mg cholesterol
124 mg sodium
1 g fibre

Try substituting caraway seeds, chopped dill or sliced sun-dried tomatoes for the sunflower seeds. This bread is best fresh out of the oven.

3^1/$_2$ cups	flour	840 mL
2 Tbsp	sugar	30 mL
1 Tbsp	baking powder	15 mL
1	12-oz (355-mL) can beer, at room temperature	1
3 Tbsp	sunflower seeds	45 mL

Preheat oven to 350°F (175°C). Line 8- x 4-in (20- x 10-cm) loaf pan with parchment paper or foil. Mix flour, sugar and baking powder together. Add beer and mix. Stir in sunflower seeds. Knead dough a few times. Fit dough into prepared pan.

Bake for 1 hour, or until toothpick inserted in centre comes out clean. Turn loaf out of pan and place on its side to cool on a rack.

Makes 12 slices.

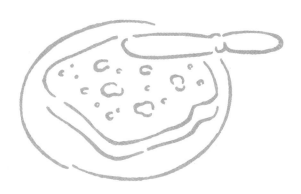

herbed cheese bread

Nutrition notes:
Muffins and seasoned breads do not need extra spreads, such as margarine, especially when they are moist and straight from the oven.

Nutritional analysis per slice:
104 calories
4 g protein
4 g fat
1 g saturated fat
13 g carbohydrate
32 mg cholesterol
664 mg sodium
1 g fibre

Batter breads are simple to make because they require no kneading.

1^1/$_2$ cups	boiling water	360 mL
2 Tbsp	margarine	30 mL
^{1}/$_4$ cup	sugar	60 mL
1^1/$_2$ Tbsp	dried oregano	22.5 mL
1 tsp	salt	5 mL
1^1/$_2$ tsp	seasoning salt	7.5 mL
2 envelopes	rapid-rise yeast	2 envelopes
4 cups	flour	950 mL
1	egg, beaten	1
^{1}/$_4$ cup	grated Parmesan cheese	60 mL
^{1}/$_3$ cup	skim milk powder	80 mL
1 tsp	olive oil	5 mL
1 Tbsp	grated Parmesan cheese	15 mL

Preheat oven to 350°F (175°C). Grease two 6-cup (1.5-L) casserole dishes.

In large bowl, combine boiling water, margarine, sugar, oregano, salt and seasoning salt. Mix well and let cool until lukewarm.

Stir rapid-rise yeast into 3 cups (720 mL) of the flour, mixing well. Add to cooled liquid mixture along with egg, ^{1}/$_4$ cup (60 mL) cheese and skim milk powder. Mix until smooth. Add remaining flour and mix well. Place dough in large greased bowl and cover bowl with tea towel. Let rise until dough is doubled, about 1–1^1/$_2$ hours.

Stir down and mix for about 30 seconds. Divide dough between two prepared casserole dishes. Cover each with tea towel and let rise again until dough is doubled in size, about 30 minutes.

Lightly oil or spray top of dough with olive oil and sprinkle with remaining 1 Tbsp (15 mL) Parmesan cheese. Bake for 30–40 minutes, or until bread is golden brown. Remove from pan to rack and cool 10 minutes before slicing. Serve warm.

Each loaf makes 8 slices.

 Timesaver tip:
If you are in a rush, but would like fresh-baked seasoned bread, top frozen bread dough with a spray of olive oil and a sprinkle of Parmesan cheese and oregano.

chocolate ginger biscotti

Nutrition notes:
Although pure chocolate contains 10 grams of fat per ounce, pure cocoa powder has only $^1/_2$ gram of fat per tablespoon (15 mL). Add cocoa powder to the cake mix when making angel food cake to make an almost fat-free chocolate cake.

Nutritional analysis per biscotti:
66 calories
2 g protein
1 g fat
0 g saturated fat
12 g carbohydrate
18 mg cholesterol
60 mg sodium
1 g fibre

Enjoy biscotti with a fresh-brewed cup of coffee for a "true biscotti experience." Add cut-up crystallized ginger to the recipe if you like a stronger ginger flavour.

2$^1/_2$ cups	flour	600 mL
1 cup	sugar	240 mL
1 tsp	baking soda	5 mL
2 Tbsp	cocoa powder	30 mL
$^1/_4$ tsp	ground cinnamon	1.2 mL
$^1/_4$ tsp	ground cloves	1.2 mL
$^1/_4$ tsp	salt	1.2 mL
3	eggs	3
$^1/_2$ tsp	almond extract	2.5 mL
2 Tbsp	peeled and grated fresh ginger	30 mL
1 Tbsp	water	15 mL
$^1/_2$ cup	coarsely chopped toasted almonds	120 mL
1	egg white	1
1 tsp	water	5 mL

Preheat oven to 350°F (175°C). Lightly grease and flour a baking sheet.

In mixing bowl, combine flour, sugar, baking soda, cocoa powder, cinnamon, cloves and salt. Add whole eggs, almond extract, ginger and 1 Tbsp (15 mL) water, beating until smooth dough is formed. Stir in almonds.

Turn dough onto lightly floured surface. Knead several times. Divide dough in two. Form each piece into a flattish log about 13 in (33 cm) long and 2 in (5 cm) wide. Arrange logs at least 3 in (7.5 cm) apart on prepared baking sheet. Beat egg white with 1 tsp (5 mL) water and brush onto logs. Bake for 30 minutes. Let cool for 10 minutes.

Turn oven down to 325°F (165°C). Place logs on cutting board and cut them crosswise on the diagonal into ½-in (1.2-cm) slices. Arrange slices on baking sheet. Place in oven and toast for 5 minutes per side, or until firm. Let cool. Store in airtight containers for up to 1 week.

Makes 40 biscotti.

cranberry almond biscotti

Nutritional analysis per biscotti:
84 calories
2 g protein
2 g fat
0 g saturated fat
15 g carbohydrate
16 mg cholesterol
28 mg sodium
1 g fibre

If you prefer a stronger almond flavour, toast the almonds and use almond extract instead of vanilla.

1^1/$_3$ cups	dried cranberries	320 mL
2^1/$_2$ cups	flour	600 mL
1 cup	sugar	240 mL
^{1}/$_2$ tsp	baking soda	2.5 mL
^{1}/$_2$ tsp	baking powder	2.5 mL
3	eggs	3
1 tsp	vanilla extract	5 mL
1 Tbsp	lemon zest	15 mL
^{3}/$_4$ cup	coarsely chopped blanched almonds	180 mL
1	egg white	1
1 tsp	water	5 mL

Preheat oven to 350°F (175°C). Lightly grease and flour baking sheet.

Place cranberries in bowl and add enough hot water to cover. Let soak for 5 minutes. Drain cranberries well and pat dry.

In mixing bowl, combine flour, sugar, baking soda and baking powder. Add eggs, vanilla and lemon zest, beating until smooth dough is formed. Stir in cranberries and almonds.

Turn dough onto lightly floured surface. Knead several times. Divide dough in two. Form each piece into flattish log about 13 in (33 cm) long and 2 in (5 cm) wide. Arrange logs at least 3 in (7.5 cm) apart on prepared baking sheet. Beat egg white with 1 tsp (5 mL) water and brush onto logs. Bake for 30 minutes. Let cool for 10 minutes.

Turn oven down to 325°F (165°C). Place logs on cutting board and cut crosswise on the diagonal into $^1/_2$-in (1.2-cm) slices. Arrange on baking sheet. Toast for 5 minutes per side, or until pale golden. Let cool. Store in airtight containers for up to 1 week.

Makes 40 biscotti.

banana oatmeal cookies

Nutrition notes:
Eating one or two
oatmeal cookies at a time
can be part of a healthy
diet, but too many can
add up to unwanted extra
calories. To help avoid
excess nibbling, keep
cookies in the freezer and
defrost them as you need
them—they will also
retain their just-baked
flavour longer.

These cookies are easy to make, easy to pack, and
a tasty change from banana cake.

$^1/_2$ cup	soft margarine	120 mL
1 cup	brown sugar, packed	240 mL
1	egg	1
$^3/_4$ cup	mashed very ripe banana	180 mL
1 tsp	vanilla extract	5 mL
1 cup	flour	240 mL
1 tsp	salt	5 mL
$^1/_2$ tsp	baking soda	2.5 mL
3 cups	rolled oats	720 mL
$^1/_2$ cup	raisins or dates (optional)	120 mL

**Nutritional analysis
per cookie:**
58 calories
1 g protein
2 g fat
0 g saturated fat
10 g carbohydrate
4 mg cholesterol
69 mg sodium
1 g fibre

Preheat oven to 375°F (190°C). Cream margarine,
sugar and egg in large bowl. Beat in mashed
banana and vanilla.

In separate bowl, mix flour, salt and baking soda.
Add to margarine mixture and mix well. Add
rolled oats and raisins (if using). Mix well. Drop by
rounded teaspoons about 1$^1/_2$ in (4 cm) apart on
greased baking sheets. Bake in oven for about
15 minutes, or until cookies are lightly browned.

Makes 60 cookies.

desserts

fruit is the best dessert!

Canada's Food Guide recommends we eat 5–10 servings of fruits and vegetables each day. Fruits are important sources of vitamins, minerals and fibre, and they are also satisfying because of the sugar and bulk they supply. Be sure to include at least 2–3 servings of fruit each day to ensure that you are getting the nutrients you need from nature's ready-made dessert.

Try these simple ways to include fruit in your diet.

- Pick berries, such as blackberries, blueberries and raspberries, when in season and freeze them to make simple desserts. To freeze apples, peel, core and slice the apples. Add a little lemon juice to help prevent browning. Put fruit into freezer bag in 4-cup (950-mL) portions to be used for apple cakes or fruit crisps. Frozen berries, rhubarb or other fruit can be used to make fruit crisps, cobblers, single-crust pies or crêpes.
- Frozen fruit itself can be delicious and refreshing. Try frozen grapes, blueberries and sliced bananas.
- Easy fruit fillings for crêpes, or fruit sauces for serving with plain cakes, can be made by combining about 2 cups (475 mL) of fresh or frozen berries, peaches or apples with 1/4 to 1/3 cup (60–80 mL) of sugar and 1/2 cup (120 mL) of water. Heat to a boil. Combine 2 Tbsp (30 mL) cornstarch with a little water and mix until the cornstarch is dissolved. Add to the fruit mixture. Mixing constantly, cook until the fruit is thickened. Use more cornstarch if a thicker product is desired. Flavour with cinnamon or lemon juice if you like. Serve as a sauce or filling.
- An interesting fruit salad can be made by combining bite-sized pieces of your favourite fruits in a serving bowl. Add 1 can of lychees (drained), juice of 1 lemon or lime, and 2 Tbsp (30 mL) honey. Serve in wide champagne glasses with a scoop of low-fat gelato for special occasions. Or serve cut-up fruit as fruit kebabs for an interesting presentation. Hollowed-out watermelon also makes an attractive serving bowl.

- Cooked whole fruits can be used as sweet endings for both elegant and casual meals. Try baked apples or poached pears.
- Fruit compote has endless possibilities. Use any combination of fruit, such as plums, peaches and pears. Add dried fruit, such as apricots or figs, for a little more sweetness and texture. Add water and sugar to taste, and simmer until the fruit is soft. Flavour with ginger, cinnamon or a splash of port to suit your taste.

chiffon cake

Nutrition notes:
One egg yolk contains over 200 mg cholesterol. Cholesterol-reduced eggs, available in cartons, contain less than $1/4$ of the cholesterol found in fresh eggs. Substituting these for regular eggs can reduce the cholesterol content significantly.

Nutritional analysis per serving:
143 calories
4 g protein
4 g fat
0 g saturated fat
23 g carbohydrate
9 mg cholesterol
192 mg sodium
0 g fibre

A chiffon cake combines the richness of sponge cake with the lightness of angel food cake. This cake has been made lighter by using less oil and cholesterol-reduced eggs. Egg whites and cholesterol-reduced liquid eggs in cartons can usually be found close to the whole eggs at your local supermarket. Ice this cake with a light glaze, or serve it with a raspberry coulis and custard sauce for special occasions.

$1^3/4$ cups	flour	425 mL
1 cup	sugar	240 mL
3 tsp	baking powder	15 mL
$1/2$ tsp	salt	2.5 mL
$1/4$ cup	canola oil	60 mL
$3/4$ cup	cholesterol-reduced eggs	180 mL
$3/4$ cup	water	180 mL
1 tsp	vanilla extract	5 mL
1 cup	egg whites	240 mL
$1/2$ tsp	cream of tartar	2.5 mL

Preheat oven to 325°F (165°C). In medium mixing bowl, combine flour, sugar, baking powder and salt. Mix well. Make a hollow in the middle and add oil, eggs, water and vanilla. Beat well.

In separate large mixing bowl, beat egg whites until frothy. Add cream of tartar and continue beating until mixture forms stiff peaks. Pour batter over beaten egg whites. Fold in gently with spatula until well blended. Pour into ungreased 10-in (25-cm) tube pan. Run knife gently through batter to remove air pockets. Bake for 1 hour. Invert cake on rack and cool for 1 hour in pan. Remove gently from pan.

Serves 16.

Optional: To make a low-fat custard sauce, whisk together 2 cups (475 mL) of skim milk, $^1/_4$ cup (60 mL) cholesterol-reduced eggs, $^1/_4$ cup (60 mL) sugar, 2 tsp (10 mL) vanilla extract, and 2 Tbsp (30 mL) cornstarch. Cook, stirring constantly, over medium-low heat until thickened.

spiced apple slices

Nutrition notes:
There may be good reason for the old saying "an apple a day keeps the doctor away." Apples are a great source of antioxidants and fibre.

Nutritional analysis per serving:
110 calories
0 g protein
1 g fat
0 g saturated fat
27 g carbohydrate
0 mg cholesterol
12 mg sodium
3 g fibre

This is a step up from applesauce and a step down from apple pie. Leave the peel on the apples—it saves time and adds valuable fibre. Serve warm and top with frozen yogurt.

4	apples, peeled, cored and sliced	4
2 Tbsp	water	30 mL
	juice of $^1/_2$ lemon	
2 Tbsp	brown sugar	30 mL
$^1/_2$ tsp	ground cinnamon	2.5 mL
$^1/_2$ tsp	margarine	2.5 mL

Arrange sliced apples in microwavable pie plate. Add water and lemon juice. Sprinkle with sugar and cinnamon. Dot with margarine. Cover loosely with plastic wrap. Microwave for 5 minutes. Check halfway through cooking. Continue to cook until apples are tender.

Serves 4.

rhubarb coffee cake

Nutrition notes:
To reduce saturated fat, serve cakes or crumbles with a low-fat yogurt topping rather than ice cream. To make yogurt topping, mix fat-free yogurt with brown sugar and vanilla to taste, and pour over dessert.

Nutritional analysis per serving:
171 calories
3 g protein
4 g fat
0 g saturated fat
30 g carbohydrate
12 mg cholesterol
190 mg sodium
1 g fibre

Use more or less rhubarb, depending on availability and your preference. More rhubarb makes a moister, but slightly tarter cake.

2 cups	flour	475 mL
$1^1/_2$ tsp	baking powder	7.5 mL
1 tsp	baking soda	5 mL
1 tsp	ground cinnamon	5 mL
$^1/_2$ tsp	salt	2.5 mL
$^1/_4$ cup	oil	60 mL
1 cup	brown sugar, packed	240 mL
1	egg	1
$1^1/_2$ cups	fat-free vanilla yogurt	360 mL
1 tsp	vanilla extract	5 mL
2 cups	diced rhubarb	475 mL
$^1/_4$ cup	brown sugar	60 mL
1 tsp	ground cinnamon	5 mL
$^1/_4$ cup	chopped walnuts	60 mL

Preheat oven to 350°F (175°C). Grease a 9- x 13-in (23- x 33-cm) baking pan.

In bowl, mix together flour, baking powder, baking soda, 1 tsp (5 mL) cinnamon and salt. In separate large bowl, combine oil, 1 cup (240 mL) brown sugar and egg. Beat until smooth. Add yogurt and vanilla. Beat until well mixed. Add flour mixture and beat until smooth. Mix in rhubarb.

Spread into prepared baking pan. Mix together $^1/_4$ cup (60 mL) brown sugar, 1 tsp (5 mL) cinnamon and walnuts. Sprinkle evenly over batter. Bake for 45 minutes, or until toothpick inserted in centre comes out clean. Serve warm or cooled.

Serves 18.

yogurt orange cake

Nutrition notes:
Canola oil is high in monounsaturated fats, low in saturated fat, and contains omega-3 fatty acids. This makes canola oil a good choice to use in baking.

Nutritional analysis per serving:
209 calories
4 g protein
5 g fat
1 g saturated fat
36 g carbohydrate
16 mg cholesterol
153 mg sodium
1 g fibre

Serve with raspberry sauce and a scoop of frozen yogurt for a special dessert.

3 cups	flour	720 mL
1^1/2 tsp	baking powder	7.5 mL
1 tsp	baking soda	5 mL
^{1}/3 cup	canola oil	80 mL
1	egg	1
2	egg whites	2
1 cup	granulated sugar	240 mL
1^1/4 cups	low-fat orange yogurt	300 mL
1 tsp	vanilla extract	5 mL
1 Tbsp	orange zest	15 mL
^{1}/4 cup	icing sugar	60 mL
1 Tbsp	orange juice	15 mL
1 tsp	orange zest	5 mL

Preheat oven to 350°F (175°C). Spray 10-in (25-cm) bundt pan with non-stick spray.

Mix flour, baking powder and baking soda in bowl. In separate large mixing bowl, using electric mixer, beat oil, egg, egg whites and granulated sugar. Stir in yogurt, vanilla and 1 Tbsp (15 mL) orange zest. Gradually add flour mixture, mixing well after each addition. Pour batter into prepared bundt pan. Bake for 40–45 minutes, or until toothpick inserted in centre comes out clean. Cool for 15 minutes on rack before removing from pan.

Combine icing sugar, orange juice and 1 tsp (5 mL) orange zest. Remove cake from pan and place on rack. Drizzle glaze over cake.

Serves 16.

banana cake

Nutritional analysis per serving:
352 calories
5 g protein
6 g fat
2 g saturated fat
70 g carbohydrate
23 mg cholesterol
252 mg sodium
1 g fibre

If you like banana bread, you'll love this moist delicious cake! The jam between the layers adds a fruity flavour. If you don't have a food processor, use an electric mixer, but make sure you beat it well for a light and fluffy cake.

1/3 cup	margarine	80 mL
1 1/2 cups	granulated sugar	360 mL
1	egg	1
2	egg whites	2
1 tsp	vanilla extract	5 mL
1 tsp	baking soda	5 mL
1 cup	low-fat plain yogurt	240 mL
2	large ripe bananas, mashed	2
2 cups	flour	475 mL
1 tsp	baking powder	5 mL
3 Tbsp	low-fat cream cheese	45 mL
2 cups	icing sugar	475 mL
1 Tbsp	milk	15 mL
2 Tbsp	jam	30 mL

Preheat oven to 350°F (175°C). Line the bottom of two 8-in (20-cm) round baking pans with parchment paper.

In food processor, process margarine, granulated sugar, egg, egg whites and vanilla for 2 minutes. Dissolve baking soda in yogurt and let stand for 2 minutes. Yogurt mixture will double in volume. Add bananas and yogurt mixture to food processor and process until combined. Add flour and baking powder and process until thoroughly combined.

Divide batter evenly between two prepared pans. Bake for 35 minutes, or until a toothpick inserted in centre comes out clean. Cool for 10 minutes on rack before removing cake from pan. Let cool completely on rack before icing.

To make icing, mix cream cheese and icing sugar until smooth. Add milk and mix thoroughly. Add additional milk if consistency is too thick.

To assemble layer cake, place one layer upside down on cake plate. Spread jam over top. Place remaining layer on top (round side up). Ice top and sides with cream cheese icing.

Serves 12.

chocolate chip date cake

Nutrition notes:
Add dried fruits to baked goods for extra fibre. When you add dates, apricots, raisins, cranberries or cherries, you can usually reduce the amount of sugar in the recipe.

Nutritional analysis per square:
152 calories
2 g protein
5 g fat
1 g saturated fat
26 g carbohydrate
21 mg cholesterol
138 mg sodium
1 g fibre

Recipes for baked goods often call for butter, but you can use a combination of oil and yogurt in most recipes without compromising the taste or texture. The end result is just as tasty and very moist. The softened dates in this recipe add moisture and flavour.

1^1/$_2$ cups	boiling water	360 mL
1 cup	chopped dried dates	240 mL
1 tsp	baking soda	5 mL
^{1}/$_4$ cup	canola oil	60 mL
2	eggs	2
1 cup	granulated sugar	240 mL
^{1}/$_4$ cup	plain low-fat yogurt	60 mL
1^1/$_2$ cups	flour	360 mL
^{3}/$_4$ tsp	baking powder	4 mL
^{1}/$_2$ tsp	salt	2.5 mL
^{1}/$_2$ cup	chocolate chips	120 mL
^{1}/$_4$ cup	chopped walnuts or pecans	60 mL
^{1}/$_4$ cup	brown sugar	60 mL

Preheat oven to 350°F (175°C). Spray 9- x 13-in (23- x 33-cm) baking pan with non-stick spray.

Pour boiling water over chopped dates. Add baking soda and stir until dates are softened. Set aside to cool.

In large mixing bowl, cream together oil, eggs and granulated sugar. Mix in yogurt. Add date mixture and blend.

In separate bowl, combine flour, baking powder and salt. Add to creamed mixture and mix thoroughly.

Pour batter into prepared pan. Mix chocolate chips, nuts and brown sugar and sprinkle over cake. Using a knife, swirl topping through batter. Bake for 45–50 minutes, or until toothpick inserted in centre of cake comes out clean. Cool in pan on rack.

Makes 24 squares.

Timesaver tip:
This cake freezes well. Freeze half for when unexpected guests pop over.

lemon pudding cake

Nutrition notes:
Egg whites contain no fat or cholesterol and are an excellent source of protein.

Nutritional analysis per serving:
183 calories
5 g protein
4 g fat
1 g saturated fat
34 g carbohydrate
27 mg cholesterol
146 mg sodium
0 g fibre

This old-fashioned dessert bakes into a cake with soft pudding underneath. Serve while warm from the oven, or reheat it in the microwave just before serving.

$^3/_4$ cup	sugar	180 mL
$^1/_2$ cup	flour	120 mL
$^1/_4$ tsp	salt	1.2 mL
1 cup	skim milk	240 mL
	juice of 2 lemons	
2 Tbsp	margarine, melted	30 mL
1	egg, separated	1
	rind from 1 lemon, grated	
$^1/_2$ cup	egg whites	120 mL
$^1/_4$ cup	sugar	60 mL

Preheat oven to 350°F (175°C). Spray 9-in (23-cm) deep glass pie plate with non-stick spray or oil.

Combine $^3/_4$ cup (180 mL) sugar, flour and salt in bowl. Mix well. Add milk, lemon juice, margarine and egg yolk. Beat until smooth. Stir lemon rind into mixture.

Add white from separated egg to $^1/_2$ cup (120 mL) egg whites. In separate bowl, beat egg whites until soft peaks form. Gradually add $^1/_4$ cup (60 mL) sugar, beating until egg whites form stiff peaks.

Timesaver tip:
Purchase egg whites in cartons for recipes using many eggs or egg whites. It saves cracking and separating eggs, and there is no waste. One egg white is about 2 Tbsp (30 mL).

Fold egg white mixture into flour mixture and pour into baking dish. Set dish in shallow pan of hot water and place in oven, making sure water does not splash into baking dish. Bake for 45 minutes, or until cake is lightly browned.

Makes 8 servings.

Variation: For pineapple pudding cake, use ¹⁄₂ cup (120 mL) drained crushed pineapple instead of lemon juice. Omit lemon peel.

cranberry coffee cake

Nutrition notes:
Cake toppings often consist of a lot of sugar, butter or nuts. An easy way to reduce fats and calories is to use half the amount of topping called for in the recipe.

Nutritional analysis per serving:
211 calories
3 g protein
6 g fat
1 g saturated fat
37 g carbohydrate
35 mg cholesterol
195 mg sodium
1 g fibre

The almonds in this coffee cake make a nice change from the usual walnut topping.

For the topping:

$^1/_4$ cup	brown sugar	60 mL
3 Tbsp	almonds, chopped	45 mL
$^1/_2$ tsp	ground cinnamon	2.5 mL

Mix topping ingredients and set aside.

For the cake:

$^1/_2$ cup	brown sugar	120 mL
$^1/_2$ cup	granulated sugar	120 mL
$^1/_4$ cup	canola oil	60 mL
2	eggs	2
1 Tbsp	orange zest	15 mL
1 tsp	vanilla extract	5 mL
$1^2/_3$ cups	flour	400 mL
2 tsp	baking powder	10 mL
1 tsp	baking soda	5 mL
$^1/_2$ cup	orange juice	120 mL
$^1/_2$ cup	low-fat yogurt	120 mL
$1^1/_2$ cups	frozen or fresh cranberries	360 mL
1 Tbsp	granulated sugar	15 mL
1 tsp	ground cinnamon	5 mL

Preheat oven to 350°F (175°C). Spray 10-in (25-cm) springform pan with non-stick spray or oil.

Using electric mixer, beat brown sugar, $^1/_2$ cup (120 mL) granulated sugar, oil, eggs, orange zest and vanilla in large mixing bowl. In separate mixing bowl, combine flour, baking powder and baking soda. Add flour mixture alternately with orange juice and yogurt to sugar mixture. Mix until well combined.

In small bowl, combine cranberries, 1 Tbsp (15 mL) granulated sugar and cinnamon. Spoon half the batter into prepared springform pan. Top with cranberry mixture. Add remaining batter and smooth top. Sprinkle with topping. Using a knife, swirl topping through batter. Bake for 45 minutes to 1 hour, or until toothpick inserted in centre of cake comes out clean.

Serves 14.

apple cake

Nutrition notes:
Whipped cream has a whopping 88 grams of fat per cup (more than the average person's daily fat allowance). Mix equal parts low-fat vanilla yogurt and non-fat whipped topping for a smooth fluffy topping with less than 5 grams of fat per cup.

Nutritional analysis per piece:
153 calories
3 g protein
4 g fat
0 g saturated
27 g carbohydrate
13 mg cholesterol
143 mg sodium
1 g fibre

This moist coffee cake makes a scrumptious dessert with low-fat whipped topping or frozen yogurt.

4	apples, peeled, quartered and cored	4
¹/₄ cup	canola oil	60 mL
³/₄ cup	granulated sugar	180 mL
1	egg	1
¹/₄ cup	egg whites	60 mL
1 tsp	vanilla extract	5 mL
²/₃ cup	non-fat vanilla yogurt	160 mL
1¹/₂ cups	flour	360 mL
2 tsp	baking powder	10 mL
¹/₂ tsp	baking soda	2.5 mL
¹/₄ tsp	salt	1.2 mL
1 tsp	ground cinnamon	5 mL
2 Tbsp	brown sugar	30 mL

Preheat oven to 350°F (175°C). Spray 9-in (23-cm) square cake pan with non-stick spray or oil.

Slice each apple quarter into 4 slices. Set aside. In large bowl, combine oil and sugar. Add egg, egg white, vanilla and yogurt. Mix well. In separate bowl, combine flour, baking powder, baking soda and salt, and mix well. Add flour mixture to sugar mixture and beat until smooth.

Pour batter into prepared pan. Wedge sliced apples into batter. Combine cinnamon and brown sugar, and sprinkle over cake. Bake for 50 minutes, or until cake is golden on top and toothpick inserted in centre comes out clean.

Makes 16 squares.

banana chocolate cake

Nutrition notes:
Brown and granulated sugar are pure carbohydrate and do not add fat to your diet. However, if you eat large amounts of foods high in sugar, calories can add up very quickly. Eat small amounts of these foods to add variety to your diet.

Nutritional analysis per serving:
160 calories
3 g protein
5 g fat
1 g saturated fat
27 g carbohydrate
31 mg cholesterol
128 mg sodium
1 g fibre

Dust this moist cake with icing sugar before serving, or serve it with low-fat vanilla ice cream.

1 1/2 cups	flour	360 mL
1/2 cup	cocoa powder	120 mL
1 1/2 tsp	baking powder	7.5 mL
1/4 tsp	salt	1.2 mL
1/4 tsp	baking soda	1.2 mL
1/2 cup	low-fat yogurt	120 mL
1 cup	sugar	240 mL
1/4 cup	canola oil	60 mL
2	eggs	2
1/2 tsp	vanilla extract	2.5 mL
3/4 cup	mashed ripe banana (about 2 bananas)	180 mL

Preheat oven to 350°F (175°C). Spray 8-in (20-cm) square baking pan with non-stick spray.

Combine flour, cocoa powder, baking powder and salt in small bowl. Set aside. Combine baking soda and yogurt and let sit for 2 minutes. Yogurt should double in volume.

In large mixing bowl, cream sugar, oil, eggs and vanilla. Beat for 5 minutes with electric mixer. Add mashed bananas and mix thoroughly. Add flour mixture alternately with yogurt mixture to banana batter, beating well after each addition. Pour batter into prepared pan. Bake for 45 minutes, or until toothpick inserted in centre comes out clean.

Makes 16 squares.

Timesaver tip:
Buy a chocolate cake mix and follow the directions for the light recipe—you don't need to add the oil! Reduce the water by 1/3 cup (80 mL) and add a ripe mashed banana.

tofu chocolate cake

Nutrition notes:
To get the benefits of tofu when there is no time to make dessert, buy the sweetened tofu, which comes in plain or flavoured varieties. Simply open the package and serve as is, or add some canned mandarin oranges or fruit cocktail.

Nutritional analysis per serving:
179 calories
4 g protein
4 g fat
0 g saturated fat
32 g carbohydrate
0 mg cholesterol
194 mg sodium
1 g fibre

Disbelief is the most common reaction when anyone discovers that tofu is a large component of this moist chocolate cake. Tofu ranges from soft to very firm. Be sure to use the soft tofu as it is most easily distributed throughout the batter.

1^3/$_4$ cups	flour	425 mL
^{1}/$_4$ cup	pure cocoa powder	60 mL
1^1/$_2$ tsp	baking soda	7.5 mL
1 tsp	baking powder	5 mL
1 cup	sugar	240 mL
1	10^1/$_2$-oz (300-g) pkg soft tofu	1
2 Tbsp	canola oil	30 mL
2 Tbsp	lemon juice	30 mL
^{1}/$_4$ cup	water	60 mL
1 tsp	vanilla extract	5 mL

Preheat oven to 350°F (175°C). Spray 8- x 8-in (20- x 20-cm) cake pan with non-stick spray or oil.

Combine flour, cocoa powder, baking soda, baking powder and sugar in bowl and mix well.

In separate bowl, combine tofu, oil, lemon juice, water and vanilla. Blend well with electric mixer until mixture is completely smooth. Add tofu mixture to flour mixture, mixing well with wooden spoon. Pour batter into prepared pan. Bake for about 35 minutes, or until toothpick inserted in centre of cake comes out clean.

Serves 12.

fruit nachos

Nutrition notes:
Regular tortilla chips contain a large amount of fat, often with minimal fibre. Making your own is simple—just crisp whole-wheat flour tortillas in the oven, break them into serving pieces, and serve with your favourite salsa.

Nutritional analysis per serving:
225 calories
5 g protein
2 g fat
0 g saturated fat
48 g carbohydrate
0 mg cholesterol
168 mg sodium
4 g fibre

Use whole-wheat tortillas for extra fibre. Check the ingredient list on the chocolate sauce to make sure there is little or no added fat.

1 Tbsp	granulated sugar	15 mL
1 tsp	ground cinnamon	5 mL
2	12-in (30-cm) flour tortillas	2
4 cups	sliced fruit, such as papaya, honeydew melon and strawberries	950 mL
1/4 cup	bottled chocolate topping sauce	60 mL
1 tsp	icing sugar	5 mL

Preheat oven to 375°F (190°C). Combine granulated sugar and cinnamon. Sprinkle evenly on each tortilla. Cut each tortilla into 16 wedges. Arrange wedges in a single layer on baking sheet. Bake for 10 minutes or until wedges are crisp. Cool.

Arrange 1/3 of tortilla wedges on serving plate. Sprinkle with 1/3 of fruit. Drizzle 1/3 of chocolate sauce on top of fruit. Repeat layers with remaining tortillas, fruit and chocolate sauce. Sprinkle top with icing sugar just before serving.

Serves 4.

raspberry pie

Nutrition notes:
Fresh fruit is the most nutritious dessert. Fresh fruit as part of a fancier dessert can still add extra fibre and phytochemicals to your meal.

Nutritional analysis per slice:
334 calories
4 g protein
10 g fat
3 g saturated fat
59 g carbohydrate
0 mg cholesterol
193 mg sodium
4 g fibre

The uncooked berries keep their just-picked flavour in this refreshing dessert. Use blackberries or strawberries with the corresponding gelatin flavour for blackberry or strawberry pie.

For the crust:

1¹/₂ cups	graham wafers	360 mL
2 Tbsp	sugar	30 mL
3 Tbsp	margarine, melted	45 mL

Preheat oven to 350°F (175°F). Combine graham wafers and sugar. Add melted margarine and mix until margarine is evenly distributed. Press crumbs into bottom and sides of 9-in (23-cm) pie plate. Bake in oven for 10 minutes. Remove from oven and cool on rack.

For the filling:

¹/₂ cup	sugar	120 mL
4 Tbsp	cornstarch	60 mL
1¹/₂ cups	water	360 mL
1	3-oz (85-g) pkg raspberry gelatin powder	1
4 cups	frozen raspberries, partially defrosted	950 mL

Mix sugar and cornstarch in medium pot. Add water and mix well. Cook over medium heat, stirring constantly, until mixture is thick and clear.

Remove from heat and add gelatin powder. Mix well. Add partially frozen berries (berries should be defrosted just enough to separate large clumps) and mix gently until berries are well distributed through the filling.

Pour into cooled pie shell. Refrigerate until filling is set, at least 2 hours.

For the topping:

1 cup	fat-free vanilla yogurt	240 mL
1 cup	non-fat whipped dessert topping	240 mL
		240 mL

Combine yogurt and dessert topping. Spoon over pie just before serving.

Serves 8.

Variations: To reduce sugar content of pie, use sugar-free flavoured gelatin powder. For a fast, very low-fat dessert, simply pour the fruit filling into custard or dessert cups and chill until set. Serve with a dollop of the topping mixture.

Timesaver tip:
Use a premade graham wafer crust. The fat content will be higher, but it is very convenient.

phyllo tarts with blueberries

Nutrition notes:
Regular pastry can contain as much as 2 Tbsp (30 mL) of shortening in one portion of a double-crust pie. This adds up to 28 grams of fat, much of it trans-fatty acids. Phyllo pastry sheets contains almost no fat on its own—the only fat component is the oil you use to make the phyllo shells.

Nutritional analysis per tart:
103 calories
1 g protein
2 g fat
1 g saturated fat
21 g carbohydrate
0 mg cholesterol
42 mg sodium
1 g fibre

All components can be made ahead of time and assembled just before serving. Use frozen berries to make the cooked portion of the filling if you like, but it's best to add fresh berries to the mixture after cooking. For a change, use blackberries or raspberries instead of blueberries.

For the phyllo shells:

4	sheets phyllo pastry	4
	oil spray	

Preheat oven to 400°F (200°C). Work with one phyllo sheet at a time, keeping the rest covered with a slightly damp cloth. Unfold one sheet on large cutting board. Spray with oil. Fold sheet crosswise in half, then in half once more. Using scissors, cut folded phyllo to make 3 squares.

Fit each square into muffin tin to make 3 tart shells. Repeat with remaining 3 phyllo sheets to make a total of 12 shells. Bake in oven until slightly browned, about 5 minutes. Remove from tin and cool on rack.

For the filling:

4 cups	blueberries	950 mL
$^1/_2$ cup	water	120 mL
$^1/_3$ cup	sugar	80 mL
2 Tbsp	cornstarch	30 mL
$^1/_4$ cup	water	60 mL

In saucepan over medium-high heat, combine 2 cups (475 mL) of blueberries, $^1/_2$ cup (120 mL) water and sugar. Heat to a boil, then simmer for 2 minutes.

Combine cornstarch with ¹/₄ cup (60 mL) water. Add to saucepan, mixing constantly until thickened. Remove from heat and gently mix in remaining 2 cups (475 mL) blueberries. Cool.

For the topping:

1 cup	fat-free whipped dessert topping	240 mL
³/₄ cup	fat-free vanilla yogurt	180 mL

Combine whipped topping and yogurt.

Fill phyllo shells with blueberry mixture. Spoon a dollop of whipped topping mixture onto each tart. Serve immediately.

Makes 12 tarts.

Timesaver tip:
Use canned pie filling instead of making your own. To add a fresh taste, mix fresh fruit into the canned filling.

apple phyllo tower

Nutritional analysis per serving:
309 calories
5 g protein
6 g fat
2 g saturated fat
63 g carbohydrate
11 mg cholesterol
127 mg sodium
2 g fibre

This impressive-looking dessert is simple to make. Have all the phyllo layers and apples prepared ahead of time, and assemble dessert just before serving.

2	sheets phyllo pastry	2
	oil spray	
1 tsp	granulated sugar	5 mL
1 tsp	margarine	5 mL
4 cups	peeled, cored and sliced apples	950 mL
1/4 cup	brown sugar	60 mL
1 Tbsp	lemon juice	15 mL
1/2 tsp	ground cinnamon	2.5 mL
1/4 tsp	nutmeg	1.2 mL
1 tsp	cornstarch	5 mL
1/4 cup	water	60 mL
2 cups	light ice cream	475 mL

Preheat oven to 400°F (200°C). Work with one phyllo sheet at a time, keeping the other covered with a slightly damp cloth.

Unfold one sheet on cutting board. Spray lightly with oil. Sprinkle with 1/2 tsp (2.5 mL) sugar. Fold sheet in half crosswise. Cut with sharp knife into 6 squares. Repeat with next sheet of phyllo to make a total of 12 squares.

Place phyllo squares onto baking sheets in one layer. Bake in oven until lightly browned, about 3 minutes. Set aside to cool.

Melt margarine in non-stick frying pan. Add apple slices and sauté over medium heat until apples are slightly softened, about 10 minutes. Add brown sugar, lemon juice, cinnamon and nutmeg.

Cook and stir for 5 more minutes. Mix together cornstarch and water. Stir into apple mixture. Cook and stir for 2 more minutes, until apples are slightly glazed.

To assemble, place one phyllo square on individual serving plate. Place a few warm apple slices on top. Spread about 2 Tbsp (30 mL) ice cream on top of apple. Repeat with another layer of phyllo, apple slices and ice cream. Top with one more phyllo square. Repeat for 3 more individual servings.

Serves 4.

Timesaver tip:
Use canned apple pie filling instead of preparing your own apple slices.

simple pastry shell

Nutrition notes:
Lard, shortening and other hard fats are high in either saturated or hydrogenated fats. Because these fats will raise LDL-cholesterol levels in your blood, using canola or olive oil in their place is a better option.

Nutritional analysis per ⅛ crust serving:
118 calories
2 g protein
7 g fat
1 g saturated fat
12 g carbohydrate
0 mg cholesterol
160 mg sodium
0 g fibre

With less saturated fat than recipes using shortening or lard, this crust is a healthier alternative to regular pie crust. It tends to be crispy rather than flaky, but it is tasty nonetheless. Make single-crust pies to keep the fat content down in each piece of pie.

2 cups	flour	475 mL
1 tsp	salt	5 mL
½ tsp	baking powder	2.5 mL
½ cup	canola oil	120 mL
¼ cup	skim milk	60 mL

Preheat oven to 450° (230°C). In medium bowl, combine flour, salt and baking powder. Mix well and set aside. Combine oil and milk in measuring cup, but do not mix. Pour into flour mixture. Stir with fork until mixed. Press dough firmly into a ball, and divide in half. Roll out each half between two sheets of waxed paper to make crust for 2 single-crust pies. Handle dough gently, as it tends to break apart quite easily. Place each crust in 9-in (23-cm) pie pan. Use for any recipe calling for single-crust pie shells.

To make precooked pie shell, prick bottom of crust with fork and bake for about 12 minutes, or until golden.

Makes 2 single-shell pie crusts.

Timesaver tip:
Serve a crustless "pie" with cookie crumbs on top. For example, bake pumpkin pie filling in custard cups and sprinkle graham wafer or gingersnap cookie crumbs on top before serving.

blackberry blueberry crisp

Nutrition notes:
Desserts do not always have to be high in fat, sugar and calories. Crisps are high in fibre, low in fat, filled with fruit and topped with rolled oats. Sounds good enough to eat for breakfast!

Nutritional analysis per serving:
206 calories
3 g protein
5 g fat
1 g saturated fat
39 g carbohydrate
0 mg cholesterol
50 mg sodium
6 g fibre

Any combination of fresh berries is delicious in this summer fruit crisp. Serve it right out of the oven with a scoop of frozen vanilla yogurt or a dollop of light whipped topping.

2 cups	fresh blueberries	475 mL
4 cups	blackberries	950 mL
2 Tbsp	flour	30 mL
	juice of $1/2$ lemon	
2 tsp	lemon zest	10 mL
1 tsp	ground cinnamon	5 mL
$1/3$ cup	flour	80 mL
$1/2$ cup	brown sugar, packed	120 mL
$3/4$ cup	rolled oats	180 mL
3 Tbsp	margarine, chilled	45 mL

Preheat oven to 350°F (175°C). In mixing bowl, combine blueberries, blackberries and 2 Tbsp (30 mL) flour. Toss with lemon juice, lemon zest and cinnamon. Pour into 9- x 11-in (23- x 28-cm) baking pan.

In small bowl, combine remaining $1/3$ cup (80 mL) flour, sugar and oats. Cut margarine in until mixture is crumbly. Sprinkle over berries. Bake for 30 minutes.

Serves 8.

Timesaver tip:
Use frozen berries mixed with flour and top with topping.

poached pears with chocolate sauce

Nutrition notes:
Although chocolates contain flavonoids that may be involved in reducing your risk for heart disease, they are still high in total and saturated fat, and calories. Eat fruits and vegetables as excellent sources of flavonoids, and have chocolate in small amounts to enhance the variety in your diet.

Nutritional analysis per serving:
284 calories
5 g protein
6 g fat
4 g saturated fat
59 g carbohydrate
6 mg cholesterol
58 mg sodium
6 g fibre

Serving whole fruit with chocolate sauce is like making individual servings of chocolate fondue. Add a cinnamon stick and a little nutmeg to the poaching liquid for a fruit pie flavour.

4	Bosc or Bartlett pears	4
1/2 cup	sugar	120 mL
1 Tbsp	vanilla extract	15 mL
1/2	lemon, sliced	1/2
2 cups	water	475 mL
2 oz	bittersweet chocolate	57 g
1/3 cup	skim evaporated milk	80 mL
1 cup	low-fat vanilla ice cream	240 mL
4	strawberries	4

Peel and core pears using apple corer to dig out core from bottom end of pear.

In saucepan large enough to fit pears in a single layer, combine sugar, vanilla, lemon slices and water. Bring mixture to a boil. Drop whole pears into boiling liquid, and reduce heat to low. Rotate pears, if needed, to ensure all parts of pear absorb some of the poaching liquid.

Simmer for about 15–20 minutes, or until pears are tender-firm. Remove pears from syrup.

Timesaver tip:
Buy canned fat-free chocolate sauce instead of making your own. Although not so elegant as serving whole poached pears, use canned pear halves if you are in an absolute rush.

In heavy small pot, melt chocolate over low heat, being careful not to burn chocolate. Add milk gradually, mixing constantly to make smooth sauce.

To serve, drizzle chocolate sauce on serving plates. Arrange whole or sliced pears over sauce. Serve with ice cream and garnish with a fresh strawberry.

Serves 4.

apple cheesecake

Nutrition notes:
There is such an assortment of margarine available that finding the right type can be a mind-boggling experience. You are on the right track if you choose a regular or calorie-reduced soft margarine that is labeled as "non-hydrogenated."

Nutritional analysis per serving:
318 calories
10 g protein
8 g fat
2 g saturated fat
51 g carbohydrate
36 mg cholesterol
266 mg sodium
1 g fibre

This dessert is scrumptious proof that low-fat desserts do not need to taste "low fat."

For the crust:

1 cup	graham wafer crumbs	240 mL
3 Tbsp	sugar	45 mL
3 Tbsp	light margarine	45 mL
1 tsp	ground cinnamon	5 mL

Preheat oven to 375°F (190°C). Combine all ingredients in bowl. Mix well. Press onto bottom and sides of 8-in (20-cm) springform pan sprayed with non-stick spray. Bake for 5 minutes. Cool.

For the cake:

1 cup	light ricotta cheese	240 mL
1 cup	1% cottage cheese	240 mL
$^3/_4$ cup	sugar	180 mL
3 Tbsp	flour	45 mL
1	egg	1
2 tsp	ground cinnamon	10 mL
1 tsp	vanilla extract	5 mL
$^1/_4$ tsp	almond extract	1.2 mL
$^1/_2$ cup	peeled, cored and diced apples	120 mL

In food processor, combine ricotta cheese, cottage cheese, sugar, 2 Tbsp (30 mL) of the flour, egg, 1 tsp (5 mL) of the cinnamon, vanilla and almond extract. Process until smooth.

In a bowl, mix apples with remaining flour and cinnamon. Stir into cheese mixture.

Pour into prepared crust. Bake for 25 minutes, or until almost done.

For the topping:

1 cup	fat-free sour cream	240 mL
2 Tbsp	sugar	30 mL
1 tsp	vanilla extract	5 mL
2 Tbsp	toasted sliced almonds	30 mL

Stir sour cream, sugar and vanilla together in bowl. Spread evenly over cheesecake. Sprinkle with almonds. Bake for another 10 minutes, or until cake is set. Let cool and refrigerate 4 hours before serving.

Serves 8.

Timesaver tip:
Freeze peeled sliced apples when apples are plentiful in the fall. Partially thawed apples work just as well as fresh apples in this recipe.

cranberry chocolate chip squares

Nutrition notes:
Brown and granulated sugar, honey and syrup are basically the same when it comes to carbohydrate content. There is really no added nutritional benefit in using brown sugar or honey rather than granulated sugar in the quantities that we normally consume them.

Nutritional analysis per serving:
132 calories
2 g protein
4 g fat
1 g saturated fat
22 g carbohydrate
16 mg cholesterol
102 mg sodium
0 g fibre

Chocolate and cranberries are a delicious flavour combination for a real treat. During the holiday season, make these for your dessert plate with an additional $1/4$ cup (60 mL) chopped pistachios.

$1/4$ cup	margarine	60 mL
$1/4$ cup	granulated sugar	60 mL
$1/2$ cup	brown sugar, packed	120 mL
1	egg	1
1 tsp	vanilla extract	5 mL
$1^1/4$ cups	flour	300 mL
$1/2$ tsp	baking powder	2.5 mL
$1/4$ tsp	salt	1.2 mL
$1/4$ cup	dried cranberries	60 mL
$1/4$ cup	chocolate chips	60 mL

Preheat oven to 350°F (175°C). Spray 8-in (20-cm) square baking pan with non-stick spray.

In mixing bowl, cream margarine with granulated and brown sugar until well blended. Add egg and vanilla. Beat well.

In separate bowl, mix together flour, baking powder and salt. Add flour mixture to sugar mixture and beat until blended. Stir in cranberries. Spread batter into prepared pan. Top with chocolate chips. Bake for 25–30 minutes, or until toothpick inserted into centre comes out clean.

Makes 16 servings.

lemon squares

Nutrition notes:
Regular pie crust has up to 1 tablespoon of fat (14 grams) in one serving of a single crust pie. Using a crumb crust made with less fat is a lighter alternative.

Nutritional analysis per square:
115 calories
2 g protein
3 g fat
1 g saturated fat
20 g carbohydrate
30 mg cholesterol
63 mg sodium
0 g fibre

For a more elegant look, dust with icing sugar before serving.

For the crust:

3 Tbsp	margarine	45 mL
1/4 cup	sugar	60 mL
1 Tbsp	lemon juice	15 mL
1 cup	flour	240 mL

Preheat oven to 350°F (175°C). Combine margarine, sugar and lemon juice and beat with electric mixer until creamy. Gradually add flour, beating at low speed until texture resembles fine crumbs. Press into 8-in (20-cm) square baking dish and bake for 15 minutes. Let cool.

For the topping:

2	eggs	2
2	egg whites	2
3/4 cup	sugar	180 mL
	rind from 1 lemon, grated	
1/3 cup	lemon juice	80 mL
3 Tbsp	flour	45 mL
1/2 tsp	baking powder	2.5 mL

Beat eggs and egg whites until frothy. Add sugar, lemon rind, lemon juice, flour and baking powder. Beat until well blended. Pour into baked crust. Bake for 25 minutes or until set. Let cool before cutting.

Makes 16 squares.

cocoa puffed wheat squares

Nutrition notes:
Every little bit counts. Add a little goodness from whole grains to your diet by using whole-grain cereals when making snack foods. Cereal, as is, can also be a quick, low-fat, nutritious snack.

Nutritional analysis per serving:
128 calories
1 g protein
3 g fat
1 g saturated fat
25 g carbohydrate
0 mg cholesterol
30 mg sodium
1 g fibre

Crispy, yet chewy, this chocolate version of an old-fashioned snack is truly a treat. Using puffed rice instead of wheat also works very well.

12 cups	puffed wheat	3 L
1/4 cup	soft margarine	60 mL
1/2 cup	corn syrup	120 mL
1 cup	brown sugar, firmly packed	240 mL
2 tsp	vanilla extract	10 mL
1/4 cup	cocoa	60 mL

Measure out puffed wheat and set aside. In large pot, combine margarine, corn syrup and brown sugar. Bring to boil over medium-high heat. Boil about 2 minutes, or until hard-ball stage. Remove from heat.

Add vanilla and cocoa and mix well. Add puffed wheat and quickly mix until puffed wheat is well coated with syrup mixture. Press into 9- x 13-in (23- x 33-cm) pan. Cool and cut into squares.

Makes 18 squares.

chocolate pudding

Nutrition notes:
Two-thirds of the fat in whole-milk products are saturated. Skim-milk products usually work just as well in puddings, baked goods and other desserts.

Nutritional analysis per serving:
154 calories
4 g protein
1 g fat
1 g saturated fat
32 g carbohydrate
4 mg cholesterol
98 mg sodium
0 g fibre

This pudding is very chocolaty and smooth—hard to imagine that it's low in fat and high in calcium.

1/2 cup	sugar	120 mL
3 Tbsp	cornstarch, packed	45 mL
1/2 cup	cocoa powder	120 mL
1 tsp	flour	5 mL
2 cups	skim milk	475 mL
1 tsp	vanilla extract	5 mL
1/4 tsp	almond extract	1.2 mL
2 Tbsp	egg whites (available in cartons)	30 mL

Mix sugar, cornstarch, cocoa powder and flour in heavy saucepan. Add 1 cup (240 mL) of the skim milk and whisk until cornstarch mixture has dissolved. Whisk in remaining milk, vanilla and almond extract. Cook over medium heat until thickened and beginning to simmer. Simmer for 3–5 minutes, stirring constantly. Remove from heat and let cool. Continue to stir as pudding cools.

Beat egg whites until stiff peaks form. Stir into cooled pudding. Divide into 6 bowls and chill.

Makes 6 servings.

Timesaver tip:
Buy packaged pudding mix and prepare it with skim milk.

orange ambrosia

Nutrition notes:
Fruit desserts provide both a sweet treat after a meal and the bonus of extra fibre, vitamin C and phytochemicals.

Nutritional analysis per serving:
100 calories
5 g protein
2 g fat
2 g saturated fat
14 g carbohydrate
0 mg cholesterol
145 mg sodium
0 g fibre

Match your favourite canned fruit with its complementary gelatin powder to make any flavour of ambrosia. Let set in individual serving dishes, and garnish with a mint sprig and a thin orange wedge for an attractive presentation.

1	10-g pkg light orange gelatin powder	1
1 cup	boiling water	240 mL
1	10-oz (284-mL) can mandarin orange segments (reserve juice)	1
1 cup	fat-free or 1% cottage cheese	240 mL
1¹/₂ cups	light whipped topping	360 mL

In large bowl, dissolve gelatin powder in boiling water. Add juice from can of mandarin oranges, setting aside orange segments. Place in refrigerator and let set.

When jelly is consistency of egg white, mix in cottage cheese. Fold in whipped topping and orange segments. Refrigerate for at least 2 more hours before serving.

Serves 6.

Timesaver tip:
For faster gelling to egg white consistency after adding juice, set bowl in a larger bowl of ice water and mix every 5–10 minutes.

raspberry yogurt pudding

Nutrition notes:
When fat-free or low-fat dairy products are used as the main ingredients in a dessert, dessert can contribute valuable calcium to your diet without extra saturated fat. Fat-free milk puddings and low-fat frozen yogurts are examples of healthy milk-based desserts.

Nutritional analysis per serving:
149 calories
5 g protein
1 g fat
0 g saturated fat
33 g carbohydrate
0 mg cholesterol
107 mg sodium
0 g fibre

Make a sugar-reduced dessert by using sugar-free flavoured gelatin powder and plain yogurt. Any flavour gelatin powder can be used with equally tasty results. Garnish with a few fresh raspberries and a sprig of mint.

1	3-oz (85-g) pkg raspberry gelatin powder	1
1 cup	boiling water	240 mL
1/2 cup	cold water	120 mL
1 cup	fat-free vanilla yogurt	240 mL
2 Tbsp	graham wafer crumbs	30 mL

Dissolve gelatin powder in boiling water. Add cold water. Chill until slightly gelled. Add yogurt and whisk or beat with mixer until thoroughly blended. Spoon into serving bowl or individual serving dishes. Sprinkle with graham wafer crumbs. Chill in refrigerator until firm.

Serves 4.

contributors

The following individuals have contributed their recipes and ideas to this cookbook:

Pat Brechin
Jane Brotzel
Anne Budge
Alice Chen
Sonia Chrysomilides
Darcye Cuffe
Betty Darragh
Noah Dolgoy
Norman Elliott
Marcia Foreman
Barbara Joffe
Mark Killas
Elizabeth Laquer
Leslie Lee
Marie-France Leroi
Cynthia Lewin
Susan Lowe-Wylde
Leslie MacIlwee
Mary McArthur
Eleanor McComb

Bonnie McNaughton
Christine Molnar
Mary Parker
Margaret Putman
Frances Ratner
Glen Rudkin
Robert Schneider
Gertrude Schnorbus
Carolyn Secret
Marianne Soltau
Donata Startin
Karol Traviss
Hannelore Vannetta
Lynne Varey
Tita White
Pamela Wolfman
Eileen Wong
Quincy Young
Jill Ziemer

index